How To Be A Twenty-First Century Pioneer Woman

HOW TO BE A TWENTY-FIRST CENTURY PIONEER WOMAN

BY NEYLAN MCBAINE

TABLE OF CONTENTS

INTRODUCTION:

FRONTIER WOMEN FOR A MODERN AGE

Congratulations, you've just cracked open a new book. Where are you at this moment as you read these opening words? Are you in your own warm bed at the end of a long day? Are you at the dining room table catching a moment between making peanut butter sandwiches for your children? Are you on a lunch break? In a dorm room? On an airplane flying to a romantic vacation? I am at my Ikea desk in our little student apartment in Boston. One kid is asleep, the other is watching Little Einsteins, and the third is kicking around in my tummy. Things are good. But could things be even better if I were sitting in a luxurious stuffed armchair typing this in a room of my own, a private place I could escape kids, dishes and clutter?

Maybe, but those luxuries would require a space larger than my little apartment; a space, say, like a house. And I've never lived in a house. It's true, I'm 31 years old, and I've never lived in a free-standing, bonafide house. I was born in New York City and raised in a two-bedroom apartment in Manhattan. Then, after college, I moved to San Francisco where home was a one-bedroom. (We had two kids sleeping in a closet before we moved!) Now, in Boston, we've upgraded to a three-bedroom, which seems just about right size to clean, keep track of toys and have a watchful eye on the kids at all times.

The fact that I've never lived in a house gives me a clear advantage when playing "I Never", the party game in which each person states something that they've never done that they think other people have done, such as "I've never been to Disneyland." Then everyone who *has* been to Disneyland has to hand over a penny or a button or an M&M or whatever the game is being played with. Well my strategy is to just sit back for a while and then when things start getting hot, I pull out my winning list:

"I've never lived in a house."

"I've never had siblings."

"I've never lived in a suburb."

"I've never attended a public school."

"I've never been to a prom."

"I've never had parents married in the temple."

So I win the game because I'm seemingly so different from everyone else. They just hand over their M&Ms and wonder how I've survived such a strange, deprived life. Honestly, it's been a wonderful life, but with some noticeable variations from the life of a stereotypical Mormon woman.

But now that you know these odd things about me, can we still have anything in common? If you and I were to meet for lunch, what could we talk about? Would we become friends? Of course we would, because underpinning both of our lives has been a dedication to Jesus Christ and presumably, if you're reading this book, to the Church of Jesus Christ of Latter-day Saints. The differences that help me win "I Never" should in no way stop us from finding connections as women and as members of the Church. Although I may have learned the gospel on the streets of Manhattan and you perhaps at loving Family Home Evenings complete with homemade treats, we have the gospel bond.

Finding common ground in our faith is the same assessment we are asked to make over and over again as we read through the scriptures and encounter people who lived very different lives from our own. We continually ask ourselves, How can I learn from someone whose life seems so different from mine on paper? As women, our job is even harder since most of the scriptural characters we study are men. What's a girl to do when she gets to Captain Moroni? What on earth can she learn from an ancient Nephite soldier who built forts?

Of course we know the answer. We look beyond the fact that Moroni was a male warrior and that we are not, and instead study the characteristics that made him great: faith, humility, dependence on the Lord. All good things, of course, that we can apply in our own lives. But sometimes it's just so nice to be able to read about the life of a woman instead, someone who may have lived a long time ago and never in a house in suburban Utah, but who still shared our same hormonal tendencies.

Who do we have to choose from? Esther is a popular exemplar (and deservedly so) as are several other Old Testament heroines. And the New Testament is well-stocked with women from all walks of life who were close to the Savior. But how about women in the Book of Mormon, our uniquely latter-day scripture? There's Abish, the servant who was instrumental in the conversion of Limhi and his wife, the queen. And there's Sarah, Lehi's wife, but she's often remembered for "murmuring" when her sons didn't return from Jerusalem after trying to get the plates from Laban. But there is a group of women we don't readily remember when cataloging the women in the Book of Mormon: My favorite female friends in the Book of Mormon are all those other women who left Jerusalem with Lehi and his sons, those nameless "daughters of Ishmael" who just picked up and left their homes to follow the prophetic visions of an old neighbor named Lehi. The daughters of Ishmael play an important role in the early Book of Mormon narrative – serving as the mothers of the nascent Nephite and Lamanite nations – but they are inevitably overshadowed by the more colorful characters of Nephi, Lehi, Laman and Lemuel.

When we stop to read between the lines, though, it's clear that those five daughters must have been full of strength and spunk. Perhaps just as much spunk as the five Bennett girls from Jane Austen's *Pride and Prejudice*. In fact, we might take the comparison even a bit further to help us add some color and character to these Book of Mormon founding mothers: perhaps Austen's beautiful and serene Jane could be paired up with Lehi's son Sam, the strong, silent type who remains faithful to his prophet father and brother throughout his family's feuding. Of course Elizabeth belongs to none other than Nephi himself (Nephi as Mr. Darcy? Hmm...), she being the leader of her sisters, the one willing to risk the most for what she holds dear. Mary, the odd ball who doesn't quite fit in with her tight-knit sisters, goes to the faithful Zoram, himself not a son of Lehi and so always a bit of an outsider. And that of course leaves Kitty and Lydia, the silly youngest sisters, who might appropriately go to Laman and Lemuel, the flighty, faithless sons who cause all the trouble.

Well it might be a stretch, but now at least we have names and personalities to go with these five pivotal ladies of scripture. And what did these ladies do? Merely act as the pioneers of their generation. They faced frontiers that would be daunting to women of any era. They left their homes and settled families in a new land. They ate raw meat, bore children in the wilderness, established new homes in an unknown land. But their husbands' feud forced them to confront the most important frontier of all, the frontier at which they had to choose faith or disbelief, righteousness or unrighteousness. They had to decide if they wanted to follow the teachings of their parents and remain faithful to the God of Lehi, or follow the resentful and rebellious example of Laman and Lemuel. At a crucial time during which they were entering adulthood, starting married life and beginning families, these women had to choose which side they were on. Some chose to follow the Lord. Some did not.

This choice, this frontier, offers us an important opportunity to liken the daughters of Ishmael to ourselves. Can we see ourselves in any of the daughters? Whose choices are we going to emulate in our own lives? Jane, Elizabeth and Mary who choose wisely, or Kitty and Lydia who choose poorly?

While women might be scarce in the Book of Mormon, tough frontier women who choose righteousness are not hard to come by when we look at the whole history of our church and the real frontier women of early church history. The pioneer women of the 19th century also left their homes, crossed new territories, bore children in treacherous circumstances and made choices to be obedient. We glean ample inspiration from them as we read their journals and hear their tales, and we wonder again how we can liken these women to ourselves.

Perhaps, as with Jane, Elizabeth and Mary, we are inspired by their dedication to the gospel and their willingness to sacrifice everything for it. Perhaps reading their stories helps us want to be more committed to the gospel too, to stand firm by our faith in the face of obstacles. But perhaps we find their lives a little intimidating too: those pioneer women travelled while pregnant, buried family members, walked or sailed for thousands of miles, left all their worldly possessions. Being a pioneer, both anciently and in the nineteenth century, seems to have meant sacrificing physical and emotional comfort in a demonstration of commitment to God.

Compared to them, what use are we to the Lord, who live in such relative splendor and ease?

Is there such a thing as a twenty-first century pioneer woman, or is it only a construct of a bygone era? If there are pioneer women today at the beginning of the twenty-first century, who are they? What do they look like and where do they live? Are they still sacrificing comfort and wealth in commitment to the Lord?

Within church culture, we have built up a few mythical indicators of a true blue modern-day pioneer woman. She's a woman whose life echoes the long suffering of our foremothers: She has lots of children (inevitably trying to bear them "without drugs"), she makes things (crafts, home decorations, clothes, quilts), and she seems to have an inexhaustible well of self-sacrificing patience. This vision fits the time-honored caricature of the perfect Relief Society sister, previously known in less politically-correct days as Molly Mormon or Dottie Do-Gooder. She is all good things, to be sure, and she seems to carry on the tradition of voluntary sacrifice. But limiting our praise of the modern-day pioneer woman to those who meet only these criteria seems absurd in a world-wide, contemporary church where women are sacrificing and showing their toughness in a much broader spectrum of ways. After all, it's cheaper these days to buy a dress at Wal-Mart than make one for a daughter, so many of the "Mormon handicrafts" of yesteryear are now more pleasurable hobbies than methods of survival. So how do Mormon women today prove our worth next to the women of the scriptures? How do we honor the tradition of tough frontier women and show the Lord we're just as committed today?

If we broaden our geographic and cultural horizons, we can certainly admire the woman who leaves the Buddhist traditions of her Japanese family to join the church. She is definitely a "pioneer woman" too. We can also admire the woman who gives up her life-long morning coffee to honor the Word of Wisdom. But what if we're one of those women who has never had to give up family, a bad habit or a home to show commitment to the gospel? Are there other ways we can be tough in our modern times without bearing the physical or emotional trauma of our foremothers?

In this book, I answer a resounding Yes! We face frontiers and choices everyday in our modern world that offer us the opportunity to be just as tough as our pioneers foremothers. Our frontiers may be more subtle, more personal, but pioneering in our modern world is a more internal challenge than it was in the days of crossing oceans. We live in a world in which our communities are made up of millions of people, not just dozens or hundreds as in the previous cultures of the scriptures, and with that plurality comes complexity and confusion. We have a vast array of options laid at our feet: varying lifestyles, competing methods of child-raising, a spectrum of career opportunities, diverse life philosophies. But if we can observe the world around us in all of its variety and contrast -- beautiful and ugly -- and still confidently choose righteousness, then we are tough! Then we are frontier women for a modern age! We may not be bearing children in a wilderness, but we can pioneer a new way of making daily choices.

The essays in this book address personal frontiers we may each encounter as we grow and progress as Mormon women. They are the frontiers of schooling, work, marriage, parenting, building a new home, developing a personality. These are frontiers I have faced myself and from my personal experiences I draw out lessons that I hope might be helpful to you. Opportunities to be tough Mormon women often come at times of transition, when, for example, we're about to leave home for the first time, or get married, or have a baby or decide who we want to be as adult. These transitions offer opportunities to make choices, and those choices are frontiers at which each one of us can prove our worth to the Lord. Let's get out there and -- with Elizabeth, Jane, Mary and our nineteenth century foremothers -- show the world just how strong pioneer women of the twenty-first century can be.

CHAPTER ONE

RELEASE AND RECLAIM

Today I read The Giving Tree all by myself. Over twenty years ago, on a pink page of a plastic Hello Kitty notebook, I wrote that. It was my first journal entry ever, and the beginning of a long tradition of documenting every success, failure, friend, enemy, pre-pubescent anxiety, pubescent crush, post-pubescent angst, argument, grade or recognition I experienced. The Hello Kitty notebook was followed by spiral-bound notepaper from school, leather binders with "Journal" embossed on the front, blank-paged books with Monet prints on the cover, and in my teenaged years, a drawing journal with reproductions of Michelangelo's "human forms" (i.e. naked people) on the front.

This motley collection is now housed in a few cardboard file boxes in the back of my front-hall closet. Sometimes I worry about how I would speedily transport all of these boxes out of my apartment if there were a fire and I had to leave suddenly, for they, truly, would be the possessions I would choose to take. Once, I embarked on a transcription process, thinking that computer disks would certainly be easier to keep with me through life than a few cumbersome boxes of paper. But enthusiasm for that project quickly waned as it took me weeks to get through Hello Kitty alone. And I realized the first-grade chicken scratch and the dramatically flourished junior high script are just as much a part of me as what they say.

Because getting out the file boxes requires moving a suitcase, the extra set of bedding with giraffes on it, and the laundry cart, I rarely read my past journals. Only when I'm moving apartments and clearing my clutter in preparation for boxing stuff up do I dig into the file boxes and pull out the notebook labeled "My Trip To India, 1989" or "College, 1995". And then I sit amidst half-packed boxes for hours, sucked into my own life's past as though it were the latest Harry Potter. And when I'm finished-- because the movers have arrived or I've simply gotten a backache from sitting on the floor so long – I feel a little more complete, and it feels good.

All over again, I meet Billy, my preschool fiancé, and Katie, my best friend from kindergarten. I open pages filled with pressed sunflower petals, with notes from girlfriends reveling in romance and joy and beauty and everything else endorsed by Jane Austen. I touch a page stained by a teardrop, pull out the program of my first piano concert. Laugh at a list of classes I took as a freshman and find in another book that I wisely dropped Chemistry (as well as any hope of being a doctor) by sophomore year.

The inevitable next step after reading my journals is to recommit myself to writing in one. And then, a few months after that, to feel guilty that the lovely new notebook I bought for the purpose of fulfilling the resolution is still sitting untouched on my desk. My justifications are thus: I share everything with my husband, and nothing interesting happens to me anymore.

I am, fortunately, in love with my husband and have been for ten years. When I met him, it was like the voice in my head I had been addressing through my journals finally found a face. And so, I talked to the face rather than to the journal. I no longer felt an urgency to spill myself to a blank page when there were 3 a.m. heart-to-hearts in which to lay it all out. And so the journal became like a best friend, thoughtlessly pushed aside when a cute boy breaks into the inner sanctum of two girls' friendship.

As I fell in love, left college, began working, and got married, I perfunctorily recorded dates and places, knowing that even if my heart wasn't in it anymore, my posterity would appreciate the information. And then, life started slowing down. No more summer trips to Italy and travel stories about which to write pages and pages. No more exhausting exams or impossible professors to complain about. No more lovesick nights or broken friendships. Soon, the computer screen at my office had more face time with me than any friend. I sat in an office chair for exponentially more time than I had ever spent on an airplane. We lived in a small apartment, we drove to work, we drove home from work, we watched TV, we went to bed. We visited relatives on our ten vacation days a year. Nothing interesting ever happened anymore.

I was, of course, wrong. I fell into the habit of believing that the only things worth recording were the definable milestones, and that I had reached those milestones and now had nothing left to say. As a Latter-day Saint woman, my years up until this point had been filled with spiritual milestones as well as educational ones. I had been taught a clear path to follow, a path that I believed defined success: A couple of years after I wrote my first journal entry, I was baptized; sometime in the midst of those dramatic teenage expostulations, I graduated from Seminary; coupled with my graduating from college was my first experience at the temple; and looking for my first job was overshadowed by my marriage sealing. Ordinances coupled with school graduations had provided the signposts I needed to make my way through life. These were the stuff of life, the things that defined progress, success, growing nearer to God, and getting to know myself.

Since my graduations and ordinances were complete, I struggled with how I should now define myself as an adult. I had always been a student, working towards the next grade in school or working towards the next ordinance of spiritual growth. The milestone of becoming a mother existed for me only in the distant future. And so, at the ripe old age of twenty-two, there was seemingly nothing else to look forward to. And so there was nothing else to write about.

Since encountering this writer's block and abandoning my journal-keeping, I've discovered that I'm not alone in this feeling that life has slowed down. Perhaps you're feeling this yourself. Maybe just a few years ago you were a hot collegiate, going to football games on the weekends and leading the local chapter of Amnesty International, but now you're home with a toddler while struggling to pay off school loans. Maybe you're scouring your singles' ward for Mister Right while starting at the bottom rung of the corporate ladder. Maybe you were a dating machine and ate out at all the trendy restaurants, but now you and your husband spend your evenings watching Seinfeld reruns and eating soup. The real life – work, money, family – doesn't give you a three month vacation every summer. The monotony, the responsibility, the seeming endlessness of it all can be depressing after years of spring breaks and state-championship celebrations.

In the United States, our cultural paradigm has most of us leaving home in our late teens to pursue college or work. College can serve as a transition time as we live in dorms or apartments and still have some financial or emotional support from home. But during college and in the years following, we make important decisions which require a mature evaluation of who we are and who we want to be.

In our country in general, the average age of mothers at the time of their first birth has been rising steadily for the last thirty years, and the number of women having children over the age of 30 has been steadily increasing. In addition, the past decade has produced a nationwide decline in the number of births. (*National Vital Statistics System: Marriages and Divorces fact sheet,* 2005) In contrast to these trends, Latter-day Saint women still tend to marry and start having children in their twenties. These differences mean that our non-Mormon co-workers, friends and neighbors approach their twenties in a totally different light: Marriage and family hardly register as possibilities in the post-college years. If they are not ascribing to the Law of Chastity, some non-Mormon peers use their twenties as a time of sexual experimentation, living with partners to test out marriage before actually committing. Because there are rarely children to support, careers can be pursued less seriously (or, for some, be all-consuming), and many of our counterparts spend more time traveling, moving from job to job or city to city than we do. As Latter-day Saint women, our goals and perspectives during our twenties can be vastly different than our non-Mormon friends'.

In contrast to non-Mormon trends, we in the Church have been asked to put family first after our educations are complete. We are asked to mature and get serious about life far earlier than our non-Mormon peers. Instead of using our twenties as a time for experimentation, adventure or single-minded pursuit of career, we are asked to condense life- and eternity-altering decisions into a much shorter time period. We are asked to take on spouse, family and career in concert with each other, rather than focusing on career or youthful self-exploration to the exclusion of all else. These events have eternal consequences and require sincere spiritual searching and guidance. Even with the help of the Lord, these are heavy responsibilities for young people.

Is there anything worth celebrating in this mess of bills, decisions, and housekeeping? Our faith gives a confirming "Yes!" As Latter-day Saints, we share the powerful belief that we are always progressing, that that is our purpose here on this earth. Our progress doesn't stop once we've completed all our ordinances or graduated from places of higher learning. Our gospel is one of joy, joy that doesn't just hover over the pinnacles of life but extends deep into its details. We understand from the scriptures and from our prophets that we can "always have the Spirit to be with us," not just when we're on vacation or having fun. The Spirit is with us at work in our cubicles, at home in our kitchens, in our cars and as we're taking out the trash.

But it's one thing to understand that adult life can be interesting, and a whole other thing to really feel it. As we leave our teens and transition into adulthood, how do we maintain that same exuberance while developing a mature sense of our grown-up duties?

Figuring that out is, I believe, the task of our young adulthood. At age thirty, I feel like I'm finally coming to an understanding of how I can maintain my sense of self and inner joy while still responsibly dealing with the demands of adulthood and the needs of my family. I'm discovering how I can maintain a mature sense of fun and adventure without missing out on my rollicking twenties. I'm discovering that, even amidst peers who aren't even thinking of marriage and think my being a mother is nuts, I can still feel young and connected to the fond assurance of my childhood. For me, the key has been to "release and reclaim," a phrase once shared with me by a friend as I struggled to define this feeling. This phrase hits home to me because it suggests that our transition into adulthood is the reorganization of existing elements, not a creation out of nothing. We each spent twenty or so years being filled with experiences and feelings: love, disappointment, work, adventures, rejection. Our formal education and our experiences at home created a complete human being, but our transition years force us to decide if that person is suitable for carrying us through the rest of our life. Is that person compatible with a new family of husband and children, or are modifications necessary? Is that person prepared to work and be financially independent, or are modifications necessary? Does that person's faith, beliefs and ethic allow her to be happy as an adult, or are modifications necessary?

Let me return to my journal for a simple illustration of this point: After getting married, I initially felt that my journal was superfluous, unnecessary because I now had my husband with whom I could share what previously went in my journal. Yet when I read my old journals, I experienced a part of myself that my husband will never know, a part of me that only I and my Heavenly Father will know. An inner voice, a perspective all my own, a recapturing of feelings as only I could experience them. While not quite admitting it to myself, my recurring resolution to write in a journal suggested that I still craved that completely personal outlet. After years of believing that I had grown out of a journal and that as an adult I didn't need one anymore, I finally admitted to myself that journal-keeping was a habit I wanted to reclaim from my youth. Not just for my posterity or because I wanted to surreptitiously keep secrets from my eternal companion, but because a journal had been a comforting tool in realizing myself as a child and could continue to help me, even as an adult.

This example uses an activity, or a choice about how I spend my time, to illustrate the process of reclaiming. But in our transitional young adulthood, the process of releasing and reclaiming can take numerous forms, such as ideologies, political views, traditions, even fashion choices. I have a dozen other examples from my own life, and I'm sure you do too: Do I want to make time for playing the piano now that I'm a busy adult, or is that no longer important to me? Do I want to use the same disciplining technique on my children as my own mother did, or do I want to do something different? Do I want to read my scriptures at breakfast like we did in my home, or do I want to read them before bed like they did in my husband's home? At this time as we're establishing ourselves as individuals or as members of new families, we are making more choices and decisions about who we want to be than at any other time in our lives.

For some, those choices are much larger than whether to release or reclaim your mother's housekeeping techniques. For me, a large part of my young adulthood has been dedicated to releasing the family structure I was raised with and claiming another.

Growing up in Manhattan as the only child of divorced parents, my life didn't always resemble that of a typical young Mormon woman. I relied on the sensitive fathers of my friends to give me blessings before the beginning of each school year; each Christmas morning was attended by a varying members of our ward family; and getting to Seminary involved walking up Broadway in the pre-dawn darkness as the *New York Times* was thrown to sleepy shopkeepers.

It was, I see now, a remarkable way to grow up. Yet as I transitioned into adulthood, I knew that I wanted to release my life in a single-parent home. I wanted to claim a more traditional family life, with a priesthood-bearing husband, the blessings of the temple, and children who loved and learned and even bickered with each other. As much as I loved having my mother as my best friend growing up, I wanted my best friend in adulthood to be my husband.

That this is the ideal was never in question. But that ideal eluded my mother, and my reality growing up was very different from that of the stereotypical suburban Mormon family. What I experienced in my own home was an alternative structure – that of a single mother raising an only child in a city—but a structure that still offered me the support and faith I needed to develop a testimony of my own.

Now beyond my twenties, I have spent the last several years transitioning from being the only child of a single mother to being the wife and mother in an active, Priesthood-bearing family of my own. This has been my largest effort to release and reclaim parts of my upbringing. My role has shifted numerous times over the past several years: from child to student to wife to worker to mother. I have occupied several roles at once and often wondered who I really am. But leaders, faith, and examples of strong traditional families have provided me with a vision of my goal, so I know what I am working towards.

I find stirring examples in the scriptures of people who grow up right before our eyes and go through similar processes of releasing and reclaiming. Ruth first comes to mind, with her famous familial loyalty. Even after her husband dies and she is free to return to her homeland of Moab, Ruth claims Naomi, her mother-in-law, as her own and commits to staying with her. In fact, the scriptures say she "clave unto" Naomi. We read her declamation of reclaiming: "Intreat me not to leave thee, or to return from following after thee: for whither thou goest, I will go; and where thou lodgest, I will lodge: thy people shall be my people, and thy God my God." (Ruth 1:16)

It is easy to miss the true impact of this story because we often focus solely on this verse alone. We may think, Well, of course Ruth wanted to stay with Naomi. They had been family while their husband/son lived and clearly loved each other. In Naomi, Ruth had a friend and a hope for a future. But if we read more carefully, we realize that Ruth was in the process of releasing and reclaiming much more than just a mother-in-law: Being from Moab, the primary god of her people was Chemosh, not Jehovah, and by committing herself to Naomi, she was officially and completely renouncing her people and her god. She was claiming a new people, the people of Judah, and a new god, the God of Israel. Later in the book, Boaz, whom Ruth later marries, acknowledges Ruth's bold release of her people.

> And Boaz answered and said unto [Ruth], It hath fully been shewed me, all that thou has done unto they mother in law since the death of thine husband: and how thou hast left thy father and thy mother, and the land of thy nativity, and art come unto a people which thou knewest not heretofore.
> The Lord recompense thy work, and a full reward be given thee of the Lord God of Israel, under whose wings thou art come to trust. (Ruth 2: 11-12)

For Ruth, this was a radical choice, signaling her arrival into adulthood perhaps even more than her marriage to Naomi's son. Alma the Younger and the sons of Mosiah are other examples of those who release immature actions of their childhoods and claim a more prudent adulthood. We see still others like Nephi, Enos, and Moroni ponder the words of their parents and decide for themselves if what they were taught was true or not. As they reach adulthood and establish their own lives, they claim truth and release what is false.

Even while taking a closer look at the story of Ruth and her relationship with Naomi, it is important to note that one of the greatest challenges to the release and reclaim process for us in modern times is the proximity of extended family in the life of a newly married couple. There is prophetic and anecdotal evidence to support this observation. The prophet Spencer W. Kimball taught that "couples do well to immediately find their own, home, separate and apart from that of the in-laws on either side." (*The Teachings of Spencer W. Kimball* (1982), 304.) He warned that if young couples do not do this, they might find themselves subject to "[parents] who hold, direct, and dictate to their married children and draw them away from their spouses...." (Conference Report, Oct. 1962, 59-60.) More recently, an article in the April 2005 Ensign by Matthew O. Richardson listed "Leaving" as the first step in establishing a successful marriage: "Therefore shall a man leave his father and his mother, and shall cleave unto his wife: and they shall be one flesh." (Genesis 2:24)

In this verse, the Lord encourages newly-formed families to release their ties to their parents, understanding that the process of releasing and reclaiming is essential to laying the foundation for adulthood. Richardson adds valuable perspective to this essential step when he observes:

This necessary step should in no way be interpreted as abandoning one's parent and family. While leaving established surroundings and relationships can be difficult and painful, it is necessary and serves a greater overall need. In fact, leaving has always been part of Heavenly Father's plan. Consider our premortal existence, for example. (*Ensign*, April 2005, p. 20)

Of course in our premortal "childhood", we agreed to separate ourselves from our Heavenly Father – or release ourselves – and come to earth to learn – or reclaim – the gospel we already knew to be true. Simply by our existence on this earth we have already recognized the wisdom in the pattern of releasing and reclaiming.

There are a number of young couples in my ward who have parents living in the area, and a brief survey confirms that their proximity can be a challenge. From my friends' stories, it's not so much any one thing about nearby parents that causes concern. It seems instead to be a more nebulous lack of independence or privacy, which means that parents' specific actions might not be at fault but that their mere proximity changes the dynamics of a new marriage relationship. Without consciously following the counsel of President Kimball, Elliot and I decided to release our own families when we decided to take jobs in San Francisco instead of my home-town of New York. By creating a new home that is all their own, young couples are forced to communicate with each other when there are challenges, rather than run home to someone more familiar, and the shared experience of confronting a new and scary place can serve as a lasting bond.

This of course must be balanced with the acknowledgement that leaving family and home is never easy and can result in loneliness, confusion and self-doubt. This is why it is so important to simultaneously reclaim parts of our youth and home life while releasing our parents. By reclaiming those aspects of our past lives that we loved or that brought us joy – the companionship of a journal, the peace of Family Home Evening, the silliness of dancing to favorite songs, whatever it might be – we retain the best parts of our experiences while still maintaining the maturity of adulthood. We are more inclined to recognize ourselves, to see our adult selves as a continuous outgrowth of our childhood exuberance rather than as overburdened adults who left childish things behind.

I've come to realize that even though my life might have slowed down now that I'm grown up and married, it did not end. On the contrary: my marriage signaled the birth of a new family life, one that builds on the education I received both intellectually and spiritually but also on the joys, habits and traditions that make me who I am. Successfully transitioning into adulthood means holding on to those big things – like the gospel – or little things – like root beer floats on Saturday nights – that connect us to our past experiences. Deciding what should be released and reclaimed is the challenge. Feeling whole, confident and happy is the reward.

Chapter Two

The First Lesson of Motherhood

Nothing has ever thrown me for a loop like motherhood. I had dated Elliot for two and a half years before we got married, so finally joining lives felt natural and welcomed. Our first years together required very little adjustment. But having a little person join our family... Well, that was a whole different story.

I was an only child growing up, did very little babysitting, and was one of those out of touch grown-ups who tried to read *Hamlet* to an eight year old. I had no concept of when children start to walk, talk, or express their personalities. Elliot, on the other hand, is the oldest of five children, and young people have always flocked to him. He can comfort a baby when her own mother cannot. Some children in our ward even started a fan club for him, complete with meetings and t-shirts. I clearly had a lot to learn.

Entering motherhood has, without a doubt, been the biggest challenge of my transition into adulthood. Some of you may be able to relate; I know that others of you will not. For some, motherhood seems to be the culmination of their education and upbringing. They seem to slip into their new role gracefully, with a perfect understanding of a mother's place in our Heavenly Father's plan, but also the ability to act on that understanding in a nurturing, faithful, loving and fun way. Motherhood fits their personalities, their goals, their definition of success. While this is certainly the ideal, it was not my reality. Despite a rock-solid understanding of the role of mothers in our eternal plan, a deep reverence for Mother Eve and a profound intimacy with my own mother, I struggled with everything from the technicalities of changing a diaper to feeling worthy of this responsibility. I had been taught the doctrine, gained a testimony of it, but now I had to put it into practice. That's where things got tough.

***

November 21, 2003

Esme screamed.

Upon first rushing into the bedroom, I took a split second to make sure the cry hadn't been prompted by a fallen cradle. Esme's cradle – a brown wicker basket with a gothic-like overhang perched precariously between two wooden posts – has slept me, my dad, an aunt and several cousins. Its design and its age prompts rounds of "When the wind blows, the cradle will fall..." from my husband, Elliot, who repeatedly gets out the WD40 to fix the squeaky hinges and tease me about my insistence on having a large, dark piece of wooden furniture looming beside our bed. "It's a tradition," I insist, but we decide that after taking a few pictures of Esme in it, it'll have to go.

Esme's thrashing was causing the cradle to sway and creak, and picking her out of it showed me the cause of the outburst: mustard-colored slime oozed out from the sides of her diaper. Holding her at arm's length, I rushed her to her changing table, peeling off clothes as soon as she lay down and revealing the extent of the mess once I'd released the Velcro diaper tab from the frieze of Sesame Street characters on the front. Every mom has a story about the first time her kid erupted like Vesuvius, and this is mine. First came the pee, bubbling up like a little spring in the ground, pooling in the plastic changing pad and sloshing as Esme waved her arms obliviously. Grabbing the green froggy towel, I mopped up just in time for the second wave of the slimy mustard. Using diapers like hand mitts, I caught the gush and deftly replaced them with new diapers when they couldn't hold any more. Six diapers later, it seemed impossible that any more could come out of such a little body, and the diaper genie had reached capacity.

"Elliot!" I screamed into the phone once Esme had been bathed, dressed and the changing pad disinfected. "I swear you've never seen so much poop!" Yeah, I said that. Once upon a time, we'd shared our

34

thoughts on the meaning of life, on Dante, Kafka and Dickens. Had it already come to this? My baby was just four weeks old and already I felt I had lost all ability for rational, intellectual thought.

Four weeks earlier, I had been hooked up to an IV, an epidural, a Petocin drip, and a catheter, with an eight pound person making her way out of me. With Elliot holding one leg and Theresa, the buxom drill sergeant of a nurse holding the other, I was finally ready to push, a process which is both ridiculous and sublime. It had been two days since my first contractions had begun, and nothing – nothing- was going to stop me now from getting this kid out of me.

Because of the blessed epidural, I relied on the peaks on the monitor screen and Theresa's comfortingly confident instructions to know when I was having contractions and therefore when to push. Esme arrived holding on firmly to Dr. Yang's finger, face up with a full head of hair. The smallest in his family at a healthy 6'4", Elliot had threatened that we'd have to put her back in to cook for a while longer if she wasn't at least eight pounds. It was immediately evident that she'd passed Dad's first requirement.

In the childbirth preparation class we'd attended a few weeks earlier, Elliot and I had watched movies of this moment, recorded in the lives of other people. I'd glanced at the assortment of San Franciscan couples also watching these intensely personal scenes – the mom-to-be swaying back and forth while headphones around her tummy played "Baby Mozart" for her negative-two-month-old, the metrosexual husband whose violently tapping foot betrayed his cool exterior – and wondered if they were feeling like we were back in ninth grade biology while the teacher pulled anonymous sex ed questions out of a fishbowl. Or maybe they were all way more mature than that and only thinking what a beautiful thing life is and what a glorious entry we all make into it as babies.

For me, it was a mix, and I couldn't imagine how I'd respond to the real thing when it finally happened to me. Now that it is all over, I've finally been able to recognize and sort though my feelings, even if they don't make perfect sense: childbirth was, for me, an experience void of elegance or subtlety, but its bizarre rawness testified to me that our bodies are the miraculous gifts we believe them to be. The "natural man" may have his faults, but only a divinely appointed mass of matter could do what I just did.

Four weeks earlier had also marked the death of a very large chunk of my pride. Not knowing how to stop the screaming machine we'd brought home from the hospital, I fed her Mylocin drops the maximum number of times allowed for newborns. I'd struggled to get out a genuine "Thank you" when I received Mylocin, intended to relieve gas, at one of my baby showers. On the list of least glamorous gifts in history, it was right up there with the Balmex, Baby Tylenol and box of 600 Costco brand diaper wipes. What good was all that stuff when my baby would only need my loving caresses to cease fussing and fall back into a sweet slumber?

Elliot's first trip to Walgreen's after we returned from the hospital produced a second bottle of Mylocin, a tube of Lanolin (since I swore I would never let our daughter – or him – near my breasts again without it), and three Nuks (an even less-attractive name for the "pacifier" "binkie" or "plug"). But Esme still screamed, and pretty soon, getting basic cable became top priority as the hours we spent bobbing up and down in front of the television – dangerously close so we could hear above the baby's shrieks – turned into days.

And so with Esme came a realization of my naiveté, my shallow assurance that I would do everything perfectly, that I would have a perfect child, and that all the horror stories of colic, post-partum depression, and sleepless nights wouldn't apply to me. After all, I had told myself, I had a pretty good grip on life so far. I can handle a kid, I'd thought, especially since millions of mothers since the beginning of time had seemed to manage. It seemed my whole success as a mother depended on my ability to be tough, to take this new experience in stride and not reveal to a soul how vulnerable I really felt.

But in private, I cried for three straight weeks. I cried at Macy's when I had to feed Esme in a dressing room because she was expressing her hunger at extreme decibels. I cried in my bathroom at 4a.m. after I'd fed Esme for the third time since midnight. I cried when Elliot came home from work and I was still in my pajamas. I cried from exhaustion, from frustration, from embarrassment that I wasn't doing a better job. Mostly, though, I cried in mourning for my past life.

It was all over, I convinced myself. Any sense of self, any relationship with my husband, any feeling of relaxation, any ability to be productive, any free time, any freedom I had ever known was gone, consumed by an eight-pound pudge ball in one of her ten meals of the day. What was this new life? Had I really chosen it? Had I made a terrible, horrible mistake? Why didn't I love my child the way I was supposed to?

Ah, love. "Isn't it amazing how much you love her?" Elliot would ask as he took her from me after getting home from work. "She's just so incredible."

"Yeah." I'd try to sound enthusiastic even though he was too engrossed in her to even hear me.

I knew I was supposed to love her. I knew my husband loved her. I knew without a doubt that this little person had been a heroic spirit, living with our Heavenly Father just days before. She was a miracle, and I knew it. But for some reason, those "love" hormones I was supposed to be stimulating by breastfeeding just weren't kicking in. Why should I love her? She'd just wreaked havoc with my body for nine months, usurped my place of prominence in my husband's heart, deprived me of any functional amount of sleep, and added a stroller, car seat, sling, blankets, hats and ten-pound diaper bag to even the shortest excursion. As far as I could tell, she hadn't done much to merit much love from me.

And that's where my perspective ended. Humiliating, wallowing, teary self-pity. And then Elliot and I went for a walk last Saturday. We walked through the streets of Pacific Heights, tree-lined to hide the magnificent town houses and Victorians crammed side by side. We found our way to Fillmore Street, a favorite hang-out for its proximity to our house, but our walk lacked its usual chattiness: there was no talk of work, of family, even of Esme. I ground my teeth tighter and tighter as we walked, convinced that Elliot was oblivious to my suffering as he pushed the stroller and periodically tucked in Esme's blanket around her.

We hadn't had a chance to really talk since we'd brought Esme home. First, Elliot's mom had descended like a whirling dervish. The mother of five, one still a teenager, Jan swooped in to cook casseroles, clean baseboards, and talk talk talk. In my stupor, I had withered in embarrassment and misery when she rocked to sleep the child who I had not managed to even quiet. I wanted to crawl in a hole when she emerged from my bathroom with a pile of cleaning rags, dirtied with the soap scum and mildew I had let fester on my tiles for months. Having my own mom around was not much better. She is an opera singer – a diva, literally – and although she wouldn't know how to clean my bathroom if she tried, she did force me on grand adventures around town.

"You can't let Esme stop you from being yourself!" she'd exclaim. "Let's go shopping!"

So we covered Union Square, Union Street and everywhere in between while all I really wanted to do was climb under my covers and take a nap.

Amidst all this, Elliot had dutifully returned to work and had even had to travel on business for several nights. And so by the time we had a chance to take our walk last Saturday, my tension had woven me into an irrational fit.

I knew I couldn't blame Elliot for anything: I knew he was trying to be supportive. I knew he thought the moms could do a better job than he of helping me out. When he asked, "What's wrong?" – which he did quite often -- I'd answer a terse "Nothing", convincing myself he really didn't care but knowing deep down I was just trying to act tough.

We reached Fillmore Street and Elliot suggested we get a bite at Johnny Rocket's. "It's a kid-friendly place," he added, and I grumbled inwardly that finding a kid-friendly place was now my dining priority.

Our silence continued as we looked at the menu.

"Neylan, are you okay?" Elliot leaned across the table once the waiter had left. "I'm really worried about you."

"You are?" I replied snidely, fidgeting with the salt and pepper shakers at the end of the booth. "You haven't seemed very concerned. You hardly pay any attention to me when you get home from work. You barely even say hello to me when you get home. All you do is play with Esme. Look at her. She's three weeks old. She doesn't even know who you are."

It was unfair, I knew. An unjustified and typically snotnosed response, but I was grateful the conversation had at least begun. Esme remained asleep in her stroller.

"Honey, I really have been concerned. It's been a little overwhelming having our moms here and all, and I've just been taking

Esme when I get home so that you can have some space. Anyway, you haven't seemed too willing to talk."

I kept fingering the salt shaker.

"You don't seem happy."

"I'm not." It was just barely audible, and the moment I said it, our smiley waiter brought us our drinks. I couldn't tell if he noticed the tears that had puddled in my eyes.

Elliot took my hand and waited.

"It just seems like everything has come crashing down around me. I don't know who I am. I don't know who that little person is in that stroller. I don't know what kind of relationship we're supposed to have now. I feel fat and old and like I'll never have another carefree day in my life. But mostly," I paused. "I miss you."

Elliot reached for the dispenser that held tissue-paper-thin serviette napkins and handed me a wad of them. I knew that anything I'd felt towards Elliot over the past three weeks hadn't been anger or resentment. It had been nothing more than sadness at apparently losing my best friend to a tomato-faced baby.

"We don't have any time together. All we do when we're together is take care of her, talk about her, watch her and try to get her to sleep. Yes, our moms have been here and they've been great and all, but I feel more alone than I ever have in my life. I can't share this with anyone. I'm going though it all by myself."

Our food arrived and this time, the waiter's smile had dimmed as he saw something was clearly going on. I tried to give him a reassuring look to tell him Elliot and I weren't fighting with each other.

"We've shared everything up until now. School, our interests, heck we even both work at the same place. We took the same classes, have the same friends, read the same books. The fact that I'm a woman and you're a man has never come between us before. But now, I'm living with this person who is entirely dependent on me for everything and I can't share that with you. I feel completely helpless and trapped. And I feel like it's going to be this way forever."

It was probably a hormonal imbalance talking at this point and I knew there was a good chance I wasn't making sense, but I didn't care. My mound of onion rings had been topped with a collection of scrunched up, wet serviette napkins, and I reached for another as the tears kept coming. I paused to see if he'd respond.

"I've missed you too, Neylan. I know I'm having a very different experience than you are right now, and I could tell that you were suffering. But listen, I've been trying to think of something that I can compare this to, something that helps me empathize with you. I think I have it. You know, when I went on my mission, I kind of felt the same way."

Elliot served in Bilbao, Spain, a mission the size of California without a single organized ward or stake.

"It was something I had always been really excited about doing," he continued. "But then when I actually got there, didn't know the language, and saw that I was going to have to live in a *piso* and have doors slammed in my face everyday for two years, it just hit me really hard. I felt like it was the end of the world cause I couldn't see past those two years. It was so different than I had imagined; so boring, so cold, such bad food and such a struggle to keep my perspective. But there were three things I decided to do that made all the difference. They might help you too."

I was embarrassed, sitting there driveling into my onion rings while getting a self-help lecture, but I couldn't wait to hear what he his three points were.

"First, don't get frustrated." I rolled my eyes. "No, I mean it. You have to decide that you're not going to let stuff get to you. You're brand new at this, and although you've done a lot of other stuff right in your life, this is tough and it's your first time dealing with it."

"Ok, second, be the absolute best mom you can be. You're like me: you're happier if you know you're doing something really well. When I was in Spain, I decided that I was going to be the best missionary there, even though I'd never done it before. I spent extra time studying my scriptures and the language. It made me a lot happier to go a good job."

I liked that one. Partly because I was overwhelmed by my new role and partly because I didn't know what else to do, my only concern up to that point had been getting by: making sure her diaper was clean and that she was fed. At three weeks old, she hardly seemed like a person to me, and I sure didn't feel like I was doing any "mothering." Mothering meant

43

reading together before bed or making cookies for school or wiping away tears and explaining the hard knocks of life. What could I do with a three-week-old that constituted mothering? I wasn't sure, but I suspected that leaving her in her swing so I could go answer a few emails probably wasn't being the best mom in the world, even to a three-week-old.

"Here's the most important one," Elliot continued. "Have a sense of humor."

Elliot's the best at laughing at life. I, on the other hand, have always preferred to wallow melodramatically when something doesn't go my way. But so far in motherhood, melodrama certainly hadn't been making me happy, so I figured I'd give his way a chance.

"You've got to laugh when you're watching infomercials at 3 a.m. while praying for her to sleep. Or when she finally does fall asleep and her short little arms are spread over her head like she hasn't a care in the world. You've got to laugh at how her face turns purple when she screams and the little tears roll down into her ears. She really is a little person, Ney, and you'll have a lot more fun if you keep it light."

It's funny how those three points have made all the difference. I don't know whether my post-partum hormones decided to give up on making me miserable or if trying to laugh really was the magic medicine I needed, but life – and motherhood—is a whole different game now. When we got home, I typed up Elliot's three points and posted them inside my bathroom cabinet door.

***

Focusing on not getting frustrated, doing my best job, and keeping a sense of humor (coupled with prayer and a few weeks of chilling out) had the same effect on me as they did on Elliot in Spain. That triumvirate was, for me, a practical guide to accessing the Spirit and to changing my feelings about my motherhood. They were the how-to manual for getting outside myself and focusing instead on my daughter, something which better women than I might not need but which I certainly did. Instead of mourning my old life, my early motherhood became a celebration of my new life: a life of service and dedication to a precious new being.

It's no surprise that what followed this dedicated selflessness was love. With time and a dedicated focus to serving my daughter as best I could, an irrepressible love sprang in me for this tiny person. I no longer asked why I didn't love her the way I was supposed to. I asked myself how I could possibly love her so much.

Almost two years later, I am amazed that settling disputes over toys, monitoring snacks, implementing a sleep schedule and reading *Goodnight Moon* a zillion times could make me more like Christ, but that's exactly what's happened. Of course it is not those actions themselves that make me more like Christ; it is the feeling that results from them. That feeling is love, and it has slowly grown into a force more powerful than I could have ever imagined. The part of me that is like

Christ – that love – would now do anything for my child, things far more extreme than waking up five times a night.

I believe that pure, unconditional love for my child always existed inside of me, but it required that I put in some effort to get it to kick in. Like Elliot suggested, I had to be committed to my role as Esme's mother, to do the best job I possibly could. And that commitment required that I focus on her, not on myself. I had to put into practice some basic principles of sacrifice and service. For that love to take root, I had to do things that demonstrated I loved her, even things as simple as talking to her, feeding her, changing her diaper. I had expected my unconditional love for Esme to be born with her, but instead, I needed to nurture it independently through daily actions. Although at the time I didn't see these actions as being divine, they sparked the divine within me.

With the perspective of a couple of years, I now feel that those simple actions of early motherhood are like ordinances. Baptism, the sacrament and temple ordinances are themselves edified versions of simple, ordinary actions. The word *ordinance* itself stems from the word "ordinary", suggesting that our most sacred rituals are simply ordinary things made divine through Priesthood authority and sacred setting. The purpose of ordinances is to bring us closer to God by having us participate in physical actions, actions that make use of the physical bodies that define our earthly existence. Sometimes those actions don't seem to be divine; we may wonder how some of our straightforward actions in the temple make us more like God, just as we wonder how changing a diaper can help us love our child. But in some amazing, powerful way, these simple actions have the ability to transfer us to a higher plane. By employing our earthly bodies and the principle of repetition, they teach us a more exalted pattern of living. They change something within us and enable us to become more like Christ.

The repetitive tasks of early motherhood may lack the Priesthood authority granted to our gospel ordinances, but perhaps the inherent divinity of parenthood imbues those ordinary tasks with their own sacredness. I believe that just as taking the sacrament every week has helped me gain a deeper appreciation and love for our Savior, so too have my motherly actions helped me to discover and grow my love for my daughter. The bedtime routine, Family Home Evening, or family meals themselves become unofficial ordinances: ordinary earthly actions like eating, sleeping and talking which transport the participants to a higher, more Christ-like plane. The actions themselves might not be divine, but the love which both prompts them and grows out of them certainly is.

Now, in the quiet moments as I sing Esme back to sleep with old family lullabies, I marvel at this little body which itself will one day serve, sacrifice, perform ordinances and feel love. Her little being reminds me that we are spiritual beings having an earthly experience, not earthly beings striving for spiritual experiences. Using our bodies for good – for service, sacrifice, ritual or for giving birth – creates in us feelings of divine love for others. And so now, after two years of developing unconditional love for my child through the miraculous process of sacrifice and service,

I come to this question: If I love my daughter so intensely simply from reading, feeding and playing with her, how much more must our Savior love us from dying for us? Simply being able to catch a glimpse of the answer is, for me, the first great lesson of motherhood.

CHAPTER THREE

AMMON IN THE CITY

My mother sold our family home in 1998, when I was a junior in college. Granted, our "family home" was a two bedroom apartment on the tenth floor of a Manhattan high-rise, but it was as much home to me as a family farm or a historical mansion passed down through generations. It was the only home I'd known, a place made sacred by the spirit I had felt there and the love that I had shared with my mom. It broke my heart to leave it. (And it didn't help that my mom was moving instead to Nebraska. But that's another story…)

Many of us in young adulthood have this in common with our Book of Mormon mothers, the daughters of Ishmael, as well as many other families in the scriptures: There comes a time when we have to leave our homes. Whether it is for college or a job or because we're getting married, at some point we officially change our address, we pack up our childhood belongings (or else they are embalmed by our mothers in a museum-like display), and we clear out to make room for a guest room, or, even worse, a home gym.

Where do we young adult women go? Where are the sands of our new frontier? Sometimes we go to a campus dorm or apartment where we let the dishes pile up for weeks and expect our roommates to take out the trash. Sometimes we live on our own and work all day so we can come home at nights and watch TV with our cats. Sometimes we move in with a new husband who wants to squeeze the toothpaste tube from the middle when we want to squeeze it from the bottom. Wherever we go, it's different from home, different from that place where the morning sun comes pouring into the breakfast room or the arm of the couch is worn from the dog's scratching. It's not that place where we knew exactly how to wrestle with the faucet so it didn't leak anymore. It's not the place where the chip in the wood floor reminds you of when you roller skated through the house before your sixth grade birthday party.

The truth of the matter is that while we're young adults, many of us women are living in apartments or dorms or even houses that are temporary. We know we won't be there long, but we're still trying to make it feel like home. The daughters of Ishmael knew that their home in the wilderness was temporary too, but it was eight years before Nephi built the ship and sailed across the ocean. During those eight years, the daughters of Ishmael "pitched their tents" and made a home in the land Bountiful. In these latter-days, we might be happy to release the midnight curfew and the family chores, but like the daughters of Ishmael, we also hold onto that reclaiming instinct: We "pitch our tent" by putting up a picture of our family or setting the table just like our mothers did before each meal. We might use the same brand of detergent or organize the kitchen cabinets the same way. We might use an uncle's old couch that he wanted to give to the Salvation Army but that we salvaged instead because we remember jumping on it as a kid. Whatever home means to us, we try to bring a little of it with us.

I think it's safe to say that for most adult women, home doesn't mean a screaming landlord and a cramped apartment in the middle of a bustling city. (I realize that I am an exception in this regard, although I don't like screaming landlords either.) But many universities, jobs, performing arts and media venues and financial centers are located in our metropolitan areas and these all contribute to drawing young Mormon families and specifically young Mormon women to urban areas. Sometimes this means a Mormon woman must make her home in a place where she can hear her upstairs neighbors and her downstairs neighbors can hear her.

Yes, these urban areas often have strong, thriving wards where the true gospel is loved and taught. (I am sometimes asked if that is the case.) If you are a young woman in such a ward, congratulations. Your position offers a tremendous opportunity for leadership and growth that you might not have in an older, more established family ward. Chances are, however, that you won't be in this ward forever. Like cities themselves, urban wards tend to be transient due to school terms, the natural movement in careers, and also because raising a family of any size in a large city requires either substantial financial means or a sacrifice of space and material luxuries to enjoy a city's numerous other offerings.

Chances are, also, that you are away from your family. You may be living alone in your own apartment, or you may have roommates. Or perhaps you are living with a "new" family: a husband, the recent addition of children who you're still getting to know. Either way, parents, siblings, grandparents and the support system you had growing up are probably no longer surrounding you.

Some of you may be experiencing an urban life for the first time, and it's probably a lot different from what you know. You may feel lonely, a little lost, overwhelmed, or just bored. You may even be wishing you were someplace else. But I'd like to propose that you are part of a divine pattern that has shaped the history of the Lord's people from the time of Adam down to your very own family: it is the pattern of building, serving, and then doing it again somewhere else.

As the church continues to grow into new cities, countries and cultures, wards like yours -- as young and transient as they may be -- will play an ever increasing role in the Church's overall strength and worldwide influence. It is essential that as the members of these wards, we throw ourselves into service to each other and to our surrounding communities, even though we may feel alone and know that we might not be staying very long.

I have lived in urban or student wards my entire life. I have rarely had the opportunity to relax as older, more experienced men and women took on the burdens of leadership, and there have rarely been large families to create a social nucleus. But these wards have been tremendous homes for the Spirit and for growth in the gospel because so many of their members contributed their all, even for a short while. These ward members understood, as should we, that in the Lord's kingdom, we build, serve and do it again somewhere else.

***

In June 2004, I found myself, late on a Saturday night, climbing underneath the dressing room doors of the Manhattan New York Temple. Audio/Visual equipment for the next morning's temple dedication service blocked most of the dressing room doors, but my goal was to reach every locker in both the men's and women's dressing rooms. Each key needed to be labeled with the corresponding locker's number, and then a spare key had to be placed in the temple's facilities closet.

That was a remarkable night in many ways. First of all, there were only eight of us that night helping to put the finishing touches on the temple so that sessions could begin bright and early Monday morning, so our small number added to the reverence of the experience. In addition to sliding under doors, I scurried through the empty halls with keys in both hands, carrying out my seemingly mundane task. The Manhattan Temple is certainly the only temple in which I can identify the facilities closet!

Aside from an unusually private glimpse into the after-hours life of a temple, I also had a remarkable opportunity to serve. Who would have thought that labeling locker keys could bring the level of satisfaction and joy that it did for me that night? I felt like I had done nothing in my life as productive as labeling keys.

But most remarkable of all is the fact that there is a temple in Manhattan at all. A brief summary of the church in Manhattan testifies to something amazing: There are currently 42,000 members of the Church in the New York area, there are 5 separate chapels within Manhattan alone, and most of that growth has occurred within the past 20 years. At the dedicatory services for the temple and at the fireside the night before, the temple was called "a miracle" by President Hinckley and others many times.

How did this miracle come to be? At the fireside, President Hinckley read from his journal and described the inspiration he received to put the Manhattan Temple within the existing stake house building. From his description, the idea for the building was clearly a miracle from the Lord Himself. But it was also a miracle that there was a group of church members in the most worldly of cities that was large enough in numbers and strong enough in spirit to make this happen.

While growing up in Manhattan in the '80s and '90s, I attend church for 18 years in the building that now houses the temple. Although I of course did not know it at the time, I saw this miracle unfold. In looking at the past 20 years in hindsight and now from the perspective of another great city, San Francisco, where I currently live, I feel that there were a number of divine principles at work in New York that Saints living in urban environments all over the world can learn from.

As the church continues to grow, meetinghouses and temples are being built in places our ancestors would have never imagined: Ghana, Copenhagen, Kiev, Helsinki. It is a testament to the urgency and prophetic direction of our latter-days, but this growth also forces us to recognize that the Spirit dwells in people of all cultures and all locations. Righteous, Christ-like lives are attainable around the globe. But how does a major metropolitan community such as Manhattan, which is not considered a haven for religious fervor, reach the point at which it's prepared for a temple?

As usual, the answer can be found in the scriptures. I recently went through the exercise of mentally thinking through all of the scriptural heroes I could, and I couldn't come up with a single one who hadn't left his home at some point to build up the Lord's kingdom elsewhere. Adam left Eden, Abraham left Ur, Moses left Egypt, Ruth left Moab, Paul left Damascus, the Daughters of Ishmael left Jerusalem, Ammon left the land of Nephi, the pioneers left Kirtland, Nauvoo and countless other places.

As comfortable as it is for us to stay in one place or be near family or have the same friends around us year after year, very few in the story of the Lord's people have been given that luxury. And many have not been happy about it. Laman and Lemuel famously lament their misfortune, pining away for the comforts and riches of their old home. Lot's wife turns to salt when she looks back at what she left behind, possibly the Lord's warning to each of us who crave the comforts of what we leave behind. The Jewish exiles of the Babylonian captivity sing the Psalm of homesickness in Psalms 137:

> By the rivers of Babylon, there we sat down, yea, we wept,
> when we remembered Zion.
> We hanged our harps upon the willows in the midst thereof.
> For there they that carried us away captive required of us a song;
> and they that wasted us required of us mirth, saying, Sing us one
> of the songs of Zion.
> How shall we sing the Lord's song in a strange land?
> (Psalms 137: 1-4)

"How shall we sing the Lord's song in a strange land?" This is an exquisite statement that exposes the nostalgia and frailty that can grip even the Lord's greatest servants. That feeling of displacement, of being torn away from a beloved home and asked to settle a new one, seems to be a common feeling among those who serve the Lord.

Unlike his infamous sons, Lehi exemplifies how the Lord would like us to handle a change of location. Instead of murmuring with Laman and Lemuel that they had to "leave the land of their inheritance, and their gold, and their silver, and their precious things, to perish in the wilderness" (1 Nephi 2:11), Lehi instead names the river and valley that make his new home, dedicates them to the Lord, and focuses on settling right in:

> And it came to pass that when he had traveled three days in the wilderness, he pitched his tent in a valley by the side of a river of water.
>
> And it came to pass that he built an altar of stones, and made an offering unto the Lord, and gave thanks unto the Lord our God.
>
> And it came to pass that he called the name of the river, Laman…
>
> (1 Nephi 2: 6-8)

We understand from the story of Adam naming the animals that naming is a divine process for establishing dominion over something (Genesis 2:19; Moses 3:19). Thus, by building an altar and naming the location, Lehi demonstrates holy signs of dedication to his new home. Although we may not have the opportunity to replicate these ancient rituals, we can emulate Lehi's admirable commitment to building a new home under the Lord's direction.

The pioneers were asked to invest time and possessions into temples at Kirtland, Far West and Nauvoo, acting as though they had settled a new home even though the Lord knew they would one day just walk away from them. The scriptures teach us there is something inherently divine in seizing a new home and making it our own; in investing our whole selves into where we are this moment and not waiting for the day when the Lord will send us elsewhere. We build and serve and then move on to do it somewhere else.

I recently thought about the willingness of the Book of Mormon prophet Ammon to fully inhabit his new home. In Alma 17, we read of Ammon's departure from Zarahemla and his touching commitment to live among the Lamanites in a land he knows little about.

> And thus Ammon was carried before the king who was over
> the land of Ishmael; and his name was Lamoni....
> And the king inquired of Ammon if it were his desire to dwell
> in the land among the Lamanites, or among his people.
> And Ammon said unto him: Yea, I desire to dwell among this
> people for a time; yea, and perhaps until the day I die.
> (Alma 17: 21 – 23)

Aside from his bold commitment to serve God in a foreign land, Ammon is also a great example of how the Lord's people can help create a righteous community wherever they are. You'll notice that in the scripture, Ammon isn't sure how long he'll be dwelling among the Lamanites; it could be "for a time" but it could also be "until I die." In the midst of Lamanite land, Ammon preaches the doctrine of the Great Spirit, protects the people and their flocks through impressive displays of swordsmanship, and generally leaves the place better than he found it. He gets to know the people. He becomes involved in their daily affairs. He commits to a life there and to helping in whatever way he can. He builds and serves. And rather than being compromised by living with unrighteous Lamanites, Ammon grows stronger as a missionary and servant of the Lord. And his community grows stronger too.

On a high level, the scriptures as a body of literature are accounts of journeys. Each of our four standard works starts with the account of a single family: the Old Testament begins with Adam and Eve, the New Testament with Mary and Joseph, the Book of Mormon with Lehi and his family, and the Doctrine and Covenants begins as the experiences of one man, Joseph Smith. But in the course of each of these books, the individual struggles of each family move outward to become the story of whole communities: the people of Israel, the early Christians, the Nephite and Lamanites, and us Latter-day Saints today. But these communities are still made up of individuals, who, like Ammon, build and serve, even if they know they will one day move on to do it all over again.

So I return to New York and the miracle that is the temple there. What is the miracle? The miracle is that in a large, transient city, there is a committed, faithful community of saints that is making a mark on the place where they live. Your city may not be New York, but there are probably some similarities: they may both be places where only a few people settle for good, where many come for education and have their sights on the future. Yours may also be a city that offers a tremendous amount to those who are adventurous: opportunities to learn, to see beautiful things, and opportunities to serve the needy. Your city offers opportunities to help those who are lonely, those who are directionless or overwhelmed.

New York didn't have an Ammon – by that I mean a single great leader who committed to a lifetime of missionary work. Rather, there have been hundreds and thousands of little Ammons who have passed through New York over the years, leaders of a smaller scale who were dedicated to serving while they were there and whose collective efforts have produced the community that's there today. Those Ammons were my Primary and Young Women's leaders, Sunday School teachers, the bishops and Relief Society presidents and the missionaries and mission presidents who served there. They were just faithful people who were on their life's journey and were committed to serving and loving the place where they lived. They were there to build and serve, and many of them, including me, moved on to do it again somewhere else. And most of them probably didn't imagine that their simple efforts would lead to a temple.

Now that I live in San Francisco, I see that this city too has lots of Ammons. Over the seven years we've lived here, we've seen so many wonderful people confront the challenges and joys of living in this place, and there have been so many who have thrown their heart into living and serving here, even if they knew they'd only be here for a short time. There have been many who have worked wonders by serving within the ward and in their callings. There have been others who have taken advantage of our beautiful location by getting involved in swimming, running, biking and other sports activities. My husband and I have joined many of the museums and attended countless performances. One woman joined a new mother's group through her hospital and shared her feelings about the church with the women she met there. There are people here taking advantage of the unusual schools this city has to offer, and others who are deeply involved in interfaith and other volunteer efforts. Others amaze me with their adventurous spirit, their willingness to explore and soak up what they can of the beauty and opportunity here.

Are you one of the Ammons in your ward? Are you wholly committed to living wherever you are and serving there and making your ward and community as great as it can be while you are there? Your ward needs you. The Lord needs you. You need to feel the stability and joy that comes from full commitment. You are a community, and if you continue to build and serve, who knows what you will be able to accomplish in 5, 10 or 20 years, even if many of you have moved on. You may be able to say with Ammon:

And this is the blessing which hath been bestowed upon us, that we have been made instruments in the hands of God to bring about this great work...

...Yea, blessed is the name of God, who has been mindful of us, wanderers in a strange land.

Now my brethren, we see that God is mindful of every people, whatsoever land they may be in; yea, he numbereth his people, and his bowels of mercy are over all the earth. Now this is my joy, and my great thanksgiving; yea, and I will give thanks unto my God forever.

(Alma 26: 3, 36-37)

The concept of Zion is the idea of a community in which everyone works together to perform the will of God and share His love (Moses 7:18). But even a Zion community is only as strong as its weakest member. In a scripture that was my ward's motto last year, the Lord says in Doctrine and Covenants 107: 99, "Let every man learn his duty, and to act in the office in which he is appointed, in all diligence." Just as my family and I have been appointed to live in San Francisco, you have been appointed to live in your city at this time, to perform callings and serve and develop your families there. What a blessing that is! We've been asked to build and serve, and someday we may be asked to do it again somewhere else.

Chapter Four

The Three-Person Couple

When I was 19, Heavenly Father rubbed his hands together and chuckled and decided to send me on a little adventure.

I was a sophomore in college, dabbling in pre-med and writing and music classes, but mostly just having a good time. My only concrete long-term plan was to go on a mission when I turned 21. I dated very little, having attended an all-girls' school until college and not being at a Church school with ample selection. I was also just coming out of my parents' grueling divorce, which followed seven years of my mom and dad living separately. Marriage, although something I wanted for my future and that I believed was divinely mandated, wasn't looking so hot at that time.

So imagine my surprise one Sunday morning after Sacrament Meeting when a tall, blonde boy, just back at school after his mission, made a beeline for me from the back of the chapel.

"Hi, I'm Elliot," he said as he practically bounded toward me.

I was sure he wasn't talking to me. I was standing next to a friend who had shocking red curly hair and who had competed in the Miss Utah pagent. My short brown hair wasn't much to look at and as I remember my outfit now, I looked liked I'd been transported from the '80s. ("That skirt showed off your legs!" Elliot likes to remind me.)

By the end of our brief conversation, I'd confirmed that he was in fact speaking to me, that he'd just returned from his mission to Spain, and that he was going to play a very important role in my life.

I'd say that it was love at first sight, and it probably was, but that would imply that we just ran off together and ecstatically got married for time and all eternity. The problem was that's not at all what happened.

Even in the midst of being in love, I couldn't shake the feeling that something had gone horribly, terribly wrong. Although I had a testimony of the theory of marriage and its importance in our eternal progression, I was detached from the practice of marriage. I didn't want marriage now. It had brought pain to my parents and seemed like a complicated, self-sacrificial situation to put myself in. Also, I was supposed to go on a mission, and not for another two years. And lastly, I was just too young. I had years of care-free fun ahead of me before I "settled down", years of feeling young, of traveling, of working in a fast-paced job, of living single and loving it. This wasn't for me, this marriage stuff. Not now.

But, being Mormon, the marriage issue came up early and often in our courtship. And Elliot was, after all, a returned missionary, programmed to pursue that next eternal goal of a female companion. And so we struggled, back and forth, for over two years: me clinging desperately to my independence and him trying to convert me to a better life of partnership. In the end, we both agreed to wait until after college to be married, valuing our educations and our youthful time at college but also preparing for a life together afterwards.

I gave up the dream of a mission and was married at twenty-two, two weeks after graduating from college, which shocked me as much as anyone. But by the time that wedding day came, I was converted to partnership, no longer afraid of the sacrifices and responsibilities. I was thrilled to be entering into this union and I felt certain it was right for me. The change of heart I experienced during those two and a half years of dating has made my marriage today one of the most fulfilling, joyful aspects of my life. The lessons of that transitional time define what my marriage is today and what it will be in the future, because it was those two and a half years that taught me that marriage wasn't just about me and Elliot; it was about me, Elliot and God.

***

Growing up as an only child, I spent much of my youth alone in my own room, reading, writing, studying, and generally being quiet and getting to know myself. I also got to know Heavenly Father, and I cherished the alone time I could spend on my scriptures and in prayer. I felt a deep and intimate connection with Heavenly Father which was facilitated by the amount of time I could spend in uninterrupted contemplation. He was my best friend, my confidante, especially since my earthly father was uninvolved in my life. He was always on my side and few earthly relationships rivaled the support and paternal intimacy I felt from Him.

When, however, I started spending time with Elliot, I felt that relationship challenged. Not because of anything Elliot did – he was wonderful at bringing his post-mission spirit and enthusiasm into my life – but simply because the time and energy I put into getting to know and love Elliot seemed to come directly out of the time and energy I had previously spent in staying close to God. It was like I had a bank account for effort spent on intimate relationships, and when my efforts shifted to Elliot, my time with Heavenly Father took a hit. Instead of sharing the inner workings of my thoughts with Heavenly Father, as I was accustomed to doing, I now shared them with Elliot. Instead of spending time alone in my room, I spent every possible waking hour with Elliot. This of course was natural to being in love, but it challenged the intensity of my relationship with Heavenly Father. How could I now maintain two intense, intimate relationships without shortchanging one or the other?

This diversion of my time and efforts away from Heavenly Father and toward Elliot made me question my romantic relationship. I hadn't grown distant from Heavenly Father – quite the contrary since I was so happy and grateful to be with Elliot – but many of my interactions with Him now occurred with or through Elliot, rather than in the solitude of my own room, and I resented that. I continued personal prayers of course, but spiritual promptings or experiences were now shared with Elliot, no longer stashed away in my private trove but colored by the interpretations and personality of another. I now had two best friends: Heavenly Father and my future husband, and I was torn between the two. I felt I would lose something if we became a threesome. But for both relationships to work, I had to find a way to intertwine my intimate divine relationship with Heavenly Father with my intimate romantic relationship with Elliot.

What role are Heavenly Father and Jesus Christ supposed to play in a marital relationship? How could I feel the same intense degree of spirituality with Elliot as I had by myself? Was it wrong for Elliot now to be the keeper of my innermost thoughts and desires? Would I as an individual remain important to Heavenly Father, or would He just see me as part of a husband/wife combo? Was it okay to spend the time growing closer to Elliot that I had previously spent growing closer to Heavenly Father? I had to answer these questions for myself before I felt comfortable entering an eternal marriage. Fortunately, the answers came steadily, if slowly.

Even if you can't relate to the feelings I've described, and my own experience of fearing marriage is completely foreign to you, I believe that the lessons I learned are crucial to helping any young woman face the new frontier of married life. Finding a comfortable place for God in our marriages is essential to fulfilling the potential of our eternal couplehood. We read and study and believe in the divinity of marriage, but oftentimes it takes practice and practical guidance to figure out how it's really supposed to work for us, and facing that new frontier can be hard.

The first lesson came as Elliot and I compared and contrasted our spiritual personalities. Just as we have emotional or social personalities, so too do we have spiritual personalities – differing ways in which we feel the Spirit, in which we worship, in which we feel close to God. I liked to throw around my testimony and my spiritual feelings in my everyday language, using terms like "blessed" and "glorious" in my common speech. Elliot, on the other hand, felt I was trifling with sacred things and preferred instead to say a prayer before he even discussed certain events from his mission. I didn't understand such spiritual reserve; he didn't understand my irreverence. Was either of us "right"? I dreamed of studying the scriptures with him every morning as we would take turns reading passages aloud; he wasn't interested, and preferred his own personal study. I wondered, would we suffer as a couple if we didn't study the scriptures in the same way?

Some of us might feel the Spirit in an emotional Relief Society lesson with a crowd of our sisters all around us; some might feel the Spirit more easily in the quiet of their own homes. Some might respond passionately to large symphonic masses and other choral works performed grandly and loudly in gorgeous settings; others relate better to the still small voice heard in a Visiting Teaching message. I have a friend who has a hard time saying her nightly prayers when her husband is in the room because of the lack of privacy; he, on the other hand, has no such issue. Is she being silly? Should he feel the need for more privacy in prayer? Another friend doggedly sat in the car Sunday after Sunday while her new husband and in-laws ate brunch at their local country club after church. Was she right to hold so firmly to what she thought were correct standards? Was her new family wrong? I myself grew up walking across Central Park with my mom on warm spring days after Church and spending a few edifying hours at the Metropolitan Museum of Art. Elliot thought attending any museum on Sundays was inappropriate. Was my family tradition bad? Was Elliot more righteous than I?

Our spiritual personalities are made up of an endless number of components: personal reactions to the Spirit, what we're accustomed to from family or childhood traditions, worship preferences, scripture study habits, and many more. I incorrectly thought that for an eternal marriage to work, my husband and I would have to have the same spiritual personality: we would have to feel the Spirit the same way, respond the same way to spiritual events, petition the Lord in the same way, study the same way. I thought that was what it meant to be of "one flesh". In a conversation before he married us, Elder Dallin H. Oaks answered my silent concerns when he told us that he and his wife never studied the scriptures together. They always studied them separately, and at different times, and that was okay. I found peace in my courtship and my marriage when I realized that, just like our emotional and social personalities, our spiritual personalities must be compatible, not identical.

Even in the best of marriages, spirituality remains highly personal. This concept is sometimes lost to us in the church because so much emphasis is put on the family and on binding the husband and wife into an eternal, seamless unit. But although this concept remains at the center of our doctrine, it should not diminish our sense of selfhood as women and daughters of God. Our relationships with God will remain individual, even private, even in the most united of partnerships. Individual spiritual pursuits can coexist within our marital unions.

Once I realized this, I no longer judged Elliot for not feeling and doing things the way I did. I started to respect Elliot's need to find spiritual answers in his own time and in his own way. We started discussing how we could meld our family traditions so that we were both comfortable with our Sunday habits. I started being more conscious of my "irreverent" language; he made an effort to share his spiritual feelings more freely with me. We began to find a way to maintain our individuality before the Lord – our personal relationships with Him – and yet still come before Him as a couple.

Identifying and preserving my spiritual personality was followed by a much more important lesson. An inspired visiting teacher pointed me to the words of Paul in Ephesians 5. Paul is considered by some to be down on marriage and his language in other epistles on the subject is somewhat discouraging. But I read Ephesians with a searching soul, looking for hope and an end to my fear, and I found my comfort. I began to decipher for myself Paul's complex metaphor of the Savior as the bridegroom and the Church as the bride, and the light bulbs began to go off:

> Husbands, love your wives, even as Christ also loved the church, and gave himself for it;
>
> That he might sanctify and cleanse it with the washing of water by the word,
>
> That he might present it to himself a glorious church, not having spot, or wrinkle, or any such thing; but that it should be holy and without blemish.
>
> So ought men to love their wives as their own bodies. He that loveth his wife loveth himself.
>
> For no man ever yet hated his own flesh; but nourisheth and cherisheth it, even as the Lord the church:
>
> For we are members of his body, of his flesh, and of his bones.
>
> For this cause shall a man leave his father and mother, and shall be joined unto his wife, and they two shall be one flesh.
>
> (Ephesians 5: 25-31)

What a complex passage! I saw no reason why the words "husbands" and "men" in this passage couldn't be replaced by "wives" and "women", and when I read the passage so that it applied to me as a woman, my eyes were opened to an aspect of marriage that I had never considered. Christ here is compared to a spouse who is married to the

Church. But this marriage has none of the self-satisfying, begrudgingly compromised characteristics that so often describe our earthly unions. This is not a give-and-take partnership, where pleasure and self-fulfillment are supreme goals. No, instead we are told that Christ's goal as a member of this union is to "sanctify", "nourish" and "cherish" his Church. He gives his whole self so that the Church might be "glorious" and "holy".

In this metaphor, Christ becomes the Savior of his Church, our Savior, because He "gave himself" for us. His perfect love for us, Paul says, is what we as wives and husbands should feel for our own spouses. We, says Paul, are "members" of the body of Christ and so we share His redeeming power. We use this power not only to nourish and "sanctify" ourselves, but we can also access it to nourish and sanctify our spouses. We can play the same role for our spouses as Christ does for us, nourishing, cherishing, lifting and blessing. What if we heed Paul's counsel and each assume the role of Christ in our own marriages? Or what if we interchange roles and view our spouses as representations of Christ in our own lives? We then acts as saviors for our spouses: we cherish them, we protect them, we forgive them. And in doing this we glorify them and sanctify them. Does this perspective change the way we love, change the way we view an eternal union?

It certainly did for me. Instead of resenting Elliot for diverting my relationship with Heavenly Father, I now put what I professed to believe (and what Heavenly Father had taught me) into action and nourished and cherished Elliot as Christ does me. I reveled in the opportunity to put away a selfish youth and assume a greater role. I saw the two of us in a triangular relationship with Christ, where each of us assumed His role to build up and support the other, to compensate for each other's weaknesses and complement each strength. My relationship with my Heavenly Father might have changed, but my relationship with Jesus Christ blossomed.

With the Savior as a focal point of my romantic relationship, I no longer feared the commitments, the sacrifices, the responsibilities. I now had a role model for who I wanted to be as a spouse. My parents' own marriage no longer loomed large like a curse hanging over me. I no longer feared losing my private relationship with Heavenly Father or my unique spiritual personality. My youth, my mission, everything I would be "giving up" no longer seemed like such a big deal. The fear of loss and sacrifice was replaced by a vision of my role as a savior. And I was now thrilled that I'd found someone who'd act in that same role for me here on earth. Perfect love cast out all fear.

I like to believe that the righteous Daughters of Ishmael understood these concepts from the start, and didn't have to learn them slowly as I did. Theirs was a family of prophets, and when they faced the frontier of marriage they were joining forces with men whose whole purpose was to be an embodiment of God. Because they understood the role of the Savior in their marriages, the righteous daughters followed prophetic counsel to flee their doomed city of Jerusalem, they protected their husbands from Laman and Lemuel's physical and verbal abuse, and they supported their husbands in extremely challenging circumstances. Even though we might not be crossing oceans and mothering whole nations, the role of Jesus Christ should figure as prominently in our own marriages today as it did in the lives of the Daughters of Ishmael. They surely had their own identities and personalities – even their own spiritual personalities – yet they each formed a three-person team with their prophet husbands and their God. Similar teams can exist in each of our homes today as we share Christ-like love with our husbands, allow them to show Christ-like love for us, and always keep our eye on that third team member.

A Catholic friend passed me a touching note on my wedding day: "What helps me keep my perspective is to always remember that my husband is the embodiment of the love that God has for me." That's what I had just spent two and a half years figuring out.

CHAPTER FIVE
LUX ET VERITAS

I knew I was at the right place. The exhilaration I felt as I walked the historic campus, the impassioned and opinionated conversations with classmates in the dining halls, the 20th Century Opera class and the Shakespeare seminar all confirmed to me that I had made the right decision.

But above all that, it was something else that made Yale the right college for me: It was the feeling I had had as a high school senior when visiting the Yale ward one spring Sunday morning. I took that feeling seriously. I had been searching for confirmation that my wish to go to Yale was in harmony with the Lord's wish for me, and that pivotal Sunday provided all of the assurance I needed.

That feeling on that Sunday proved to be a harbinger of the spiritual feelings I would continue to have throughout my Yale education.

The highlights of my college years included the dedication of the Wilford Woodruff Building (the Institute and chapel next door to the university president's home), seeing several fellow undergraduates study the gospel and join the church, and the late night discussions with my Jewish, Catholic and Muslim roommates. But above all, I treasure the early morning (well, early for college students) Institute classes taught by a lawyer who, in something of a mid-life crisis, had moved his family to Connecticut so he could pursue a master's degree at Yale's Divinity School.

When I decided to attend Yale, many Mormons not acquainted with me questioned my decision. They asked how I could put my testimony in such jeopardy by attending a non-church school. Wasn't I worried about not meeting any LDS men? How did I know I wasn't going to be drinking and sleeping around as soon as I escaped my parental overseers?

While these questions were well-meaning and legitimate, they didn't occur to those people who knew me well. Growing up in Manhattan, I thrived on being "peculiar": I had been the only Mormon in my school and I felt I had a unique influence on my classmates and teachers since I was the only Mormon many of them had ever known. I had tight relationships with my Church leaders and friends, and the Church had been ingrained into the daily tapestry of my life. Above all, I feel like I have been blessed with the gift of faith: The fact that I believe has never been in question for me and it didn't seem logical that I would have a spiritual crisis at a university that was not that different from the environment I was already used to. My testimony was not something I was going to release as I grew up. I also knew myself well enough to know that I did not want to pursue education for my own self-aggrandizement. In perhaps overstated teenaged exuberance, my one stated goal for my education was to make myself useful: to those around me, to the Lord and to my larger community. I wanted desperately to make a difference.

The Lord knew Yale was right for me spiritually as well as intellectually, and I knew it too. Yale's motto is "Lux et Veritas", "Light and Truth" in Latin, inscribed above the many ivy-clad arches of the campus. I took from this my personal motto, from Doctrine & Covenants 93: "The glory of God is intelligence, or, in other words, light and truth" (D&C 93:118). I figured that my personal spiritual studies would give me light and my Yale studies would give me truth. Not a bad combination.

My four years there passed without any challenge to my testimony. Quite the contrary. What I didn't know was that the spiritual crisis of my education would come after I left Yale and was sent into the world with much fanfare and promise. After all, our country's last three presidents went to Yale, and each one of us graduating was expected to add to that list. Instead, I left college without much professional direction. I hadn't excelled at anything in particular, and no great revelation had told me what I was now supposed to "be". My soon-to-be-husband Elliot and I felt we should start our lives in San Francisco, where I had no job prospects.

After some false starts as a paralegal and a freelance writer, I established a respectable career in retail marketing. While it was a career indicative of what most college graduates are doing in their mid-twenties, it fell far short of my own expectations for myself. I've never figured out what it is exactly I had in mind for myself. It wasn't President of the United States, but it wasn't sitting in front of Excel spreadsheets for ten hours a day either. I was supposed to be doing something really meaningful at this point, but neither Elliot nor I felt emotionally or financially prepared for children at that time so that wasn't the answer. Like the Daughters of Ishmael and so many others before me, I was facing a new frontier, the lands of a new country that I had no idea how to conquer. I asked the questions typical of so many young adult women: Who am I? How am I contributing? What is my purpose?

I felt abandoned, by my education and also by Heavenly Father who was supposed to have shown me the way to greatness. Why did I feel so strongly about going to Yale – about paying all the money, about remaining "peculiar" socially, about working so hard – if I was just going to have an average career? I had invested so heavily in myself with the one desire of being useful, to the Lord and to the larger community. Why did I feel so useless? With this great educational opportunity I had had, why wasn't I making a bigger difference in people's lives?

Believe it or not, this was a spiritual crisis for me. I confronted these inner demons again when I decided to stay home with my daughter, Esme, and be a full-time mom. Again, I hit a frontier and the transition forced me to reflect. I struggled with the knowledge that so much time, effort, money and expectation went into my education and all that resulted was an unremarkable six-year career. Was my education really worth all that? And what do I do with it now?

While your experience with your formal schooling might be different than mine, our time as young adults offers each of us the opportunity to consider the value of the 12+ years of formal education that defined our lives up until this point. We all come to the point – whether at a formal college graduation or not – where we each need to decide what the next season of life holds for us. As young adult women, this time in our lives offers us natural frontiers and the end of our college education is perhaps one of the most daunting. For some, the post-college period holds more school, additional training for a chosen career. For others, this is a time to jump right into full-time work, or perhaps a continuation of work started while at school. Perhaps more schooling comes later, or perhaps not. Some who are already married might decide to start right in on having a family, with the woman preparing for the child and never working outside the home. These are all viable models, but they share a common thread: Whereas education up until this point was mandatory or expected or at least ideal, formal schooling beyond this point is often at our own discretion.

This sudden freedom from the binds of our socially accepted educational system can be disorienting. We're offered the opportunity to release the educational focus that has directed our lives up until this point, and claim something else instead: a job, motherhood, a year as a ski bum. Whatever it is, we decide from now on how we will be spending our time, our money, our efforts. In my own education, I went to one school for first through twelfth grades, and another school for all of college. While this is highly unusual, it partially explains why I was a total basket case in my post-college years. But even if you did attend more than two schools in your career as a student, it is possible that the most challenging decision you had to make was what to major in or what sports team to try out for. But now the decisions get tougher, and our only guidance counselor is the Lord.

The transition from student to worker breeds a legion of silent sufferers as people question what their next move should be. Endless questions plague us: Have I received enough schooling for what I want to accomplish in life? Am I well enough equipped to have a career that can support my family? Should I continue with schooling even if I go into debt? Do I have a job that can pay off the debt I already have? Will more education make me a better spouse and parent? I can't afford college or graduate school; is it worth the financial sacrifice? How can I continue to learn and educate myself outside of the formal school system?

All of these questions could boil down to this: Is it time for me to release my formal education and if so, what should I claim instead?

For Mormon women, there are additional concerns: My goal is to be a mother; do I need to pursue a formal education if I'm not planning to support a family? I'm already a mother; do I really need to finish college?

Should I pursue the graduate degree I've always wanted even if I never use the acquired skills to make money? As a single woman, shouldn't I put off a graduate degree in case I get married? If I attend a graduate program but don't enter the work force, am I taking away an educational opportunity from a man who might need that degree to support his family?

I have heard all of these questions asked by young Mormon women. As an answer, I suggest we take a look at the larger role of education and learning within the Lord's kingdom here on earth. It was looking at education through the Lord's eyes that helped me snap out of my own post-college wallowing, and I believe that as Mormon women training ourselves and our children to serve the Lord, understanding the true role of education can be one of our greatest earthly acquisitions.

***

Recently a friend related a conversation she had with her Young Women's class. As the teacher, my friend asked the class why it was important for them to get an education. One girl finally piped up, "In case my husband dies and I have to support myself." The other girls nodded in agreement.

While this is certainly one answer to the question (and I do know a young mother in my ward who was tragically widowed and returned to work to support her family), this is statistically and spiritually a short-sighted answer. Statistically, it is unlikely we will be widowed while we still have young children. Fortunately that doesn't happen to that many people, and if that really is the reason young women are going to school, then they will be relieved indeed (or disappointed!). However, it *is* statistically probable that, even despite best efforts, a woman will work outside her home at some point in her life. The uncertainties of life, the varying seasons of our life, and quite simply our desire to work professionally might put us in a situation where education is required. Women work before they get married, while they're married but before children, while raising children due to financial needs or emotional health, or when children leave the home. It is far more likely that a husband will lose his job at some point than that he will die. It is more likely that they will get divorced than that he will die. It is more likely that a woman will have trouble getting pregnant and will want to work than it is that her husband will die. And it is far more likely that a woman will crave something outside the home after her children are gone than that her husband will die.

Statistically, it is also unlikely that any pre-professional skills a young woman learns in school—such as accounting, computer science, graphic design – will still be applicable if she tries to enter the work force far beyond her graduation date. Think about the way the workplace functioned ten or fifteen years ago; there was no email, for instance! Accountants learned different regulations, computer science hardly existed as a main-stream discipline, and graphic design still used paper and pencil. With technological advances progressing at the speed that they are, traditional tax filing will be outsourced to India, Windows will have been replaced by some new operating system, and Photoshop and Illustrator will be obsolete in ten years. If a young woman needs to enter the work force later in life, additional schooling will probably be required anyway for any sort of skilled labor.

So, practically speaking, my friend's Young Women's answer is unrealistic. Spiritually, it is devastating. The answer suggests that the young women consider education to be a means to a job, no more. This is a trap that many of us fall into; after all, it was this attitude that contributed to my own post-college crisis. Our culture's collective subconscious is programmed to equate education with usefulness in society, meaning that it doesn't support education for education's sake alone. Instead, it expects something in return: contributions to the community in the form of services (doctor, lawyer, librarian), innovation (researchers, engineers) or culture (artists, musicians). Gone are the days when an enlightened man (or woman), a renaissance man (or woman), or a gentleman (or woman) were achievements in their own right, essential components of a productive society because of their contributions to character and thought. The goal now (particularly in our country it seems) is to produce so as to forward the financial health of ourselves and our larger community.

These of course are broad generalizations, but they serve to underscore the root of the confusion between our earthly, culturally programmed definition of education and the Lord's definition. To fully comprehend the Lord's definition, we need to lift ourselves out of our world of degrees and paychecks, and look instead to our eternal goals. This is very hard to do because here on earth, we can never fully escape the need to use our education to make money and support our families, whether this is a task of our own or of our husband's. But by looking at the Lord's kingdom rather than to our own society, we can start to catch a glimpse of our education's true potential.

In 1833, Joseph Smith was commanded to start his own school, the School of the Prophets, while the Saints were established in Kirtland. The School served as a prototype, a perfect example of what divine education should be. In Doctrine & Covenants 88, we read that the purpose of the School was to prepare the leaders of the young church so that they could "magnify the calling whereunto I have called you..." (D&C 88:80).

Teach ye diligently... that you may be instructed more perfectly in theory, in principle, in doctrine, in the law of the gospel, in all things that pertain unto the kingdom of God, that are expedient for you to understand;

Of things both in heaven and in the earth, and under the earth; things which have been, things which are, things which must shortly come to pass; things which are at home, things which are abroad; the wars and the perplexities of the nations, and the judgments which are on the land; and a knowledge also of countries and of kingdoms…. (D&C 88:78-79)

If this course of study is to be followed literally, it must include astronomy, agronomy, geology, mineralogy, history, current events, domestic and foreign affairs, geography and language. And Joseph's school did cover many of these subjects, including Hebrew, Greek, Latin and of course, theology.

What does this example mean to us? I have found that we often segregate our educations: one bucket for "secular" and one bucket for "spiritual". We tend to default to the belief that secular education is necessary for our success here on earth, and spiritual education is necessary for our success in the world to come. The first lesson of the School of the Prophets is that this distinction is false. In preparing his servants, the Lord commanded Joseph to study a broad range of earthly as well as spiritual subjects.

A closer look at the modern Church also challenges this distinction. After, perhaps, the funds and resources devoted to our temporal welfare programs, no other Church initiative receives more attention than our education programs. Sunday School, Relief Society and Priesthood meetings, while not essential to our Sunday worship which concludes with the Sacrament, are included as part of our required church "block" because of their emphasis on our education. Seminary, Institute and the entire Church Educational System also support the education of the members. Firesides, Enrichment nights and Family Home Evenings are specifically set aside for this same purpose. And of course the temple stands as our source of supreme learning. But the Church's secular school system is also extensive: Brigham Young University is now in three locations (Provo, Idaho and Hawaii) and the Perpetual Education Fund stands as another testament to the Church's dedication to educating its members. This impressive network is the legacy of the School of the Prophets, and like Joseph's school, both theological and earthly subjects are valued.

Statistics show that all of these resources have created a highly educated population within our Church membership. In fact, the Mormon population in the United States has higher education levels than the US population in general. A report entitled "Education, Scholarship and Mormonism" by Scott Gordon shows that 53.5% of LDS males have a post-high school education, compared to 36.5% of the US, while 44.3% of LDS females have a post-high school education, compared to 27.7% of the US population in general. (*Education, Scholarship and Mormonism,* by Scott Gordon)

The Church understands the specific importance of educating women. Although our divine role as mothers suggests our work will mostly be done in the home, the Church promotes equal educational and professional training opportunities for both men and women. Never has any of our modern Church schools discriminated against women or discouraged us from attending; on the contrary, all of the Church-sponsored educational programs previously mentioned equally support men and women, and education for all remains one of the hallmarks of our Church's global efforts. Worldwide, two-thirds of all illiterate people are women. Global relief organizations such as UNICEF and the United Nations have targeted programs to help promote the education of girls in developing countries. Dr. Paula Dobriansky, Under Secretary for Democracy and Global Affairs at UN headquarters, spoke in September of 2006 on behalf of The United Nations Girls' Education Initiative: "In much of the developing world, girls represent an untapped resource and a hope for the future. Educating girls is a crucial component of building a foundation for democracy, and a prerequisite for creating and sustaining free, open, prosperous societies. Nations that marginalize half of their population cannot function and thrive as full democracies. Nor can countries that ignore this vital source of human capital be competitive in today's globalized economy." (*The Education of Girls in the Developing World*, September 2006) United Nations Secretary-General Kofi Annan has supported this claim: "No other policy is as likely to raise economic productivity, lower infant and maternal mortality, improve nutrition, promote health... and increase the chances of education for the next generation. Let us invest in women and girls."

But because we are blessed to live in a first-world country where democracy does flourish and health and nutrition are provided for, we have the luxury of investing in education that not only fulfills economic needs, but also fills spiritual and emotional needs. We can invest in learning that promotes personal fulfillment and enrichment, learning that gives us skills beyond just a professional training. We can invest in the process of *becoming*, rather than just in the gathering of information. If we, who are blessed to live in this place and time, consider our educations to be a means to information – pure facts that add to our mental libraries – then we are missing the Lord's vision. The scriptures do not praise the the rote accumulation of facts; in fact, we know that the Lord's greatest servants have historically had little formal knowledge of academic subjects. The Savior chose fishermen as his partners, and shepherds and farm boys have risen to be kings and prophets. Rather, study of the world around us – secular, or earthly, study – complements our spiritual educations to create in us a power for good. President Kimball described it this way: "…Secular knowledge can be most helpful to the children of our Father in Heaven who, having placed first things first, have found and are living those truths which lead one to eternal life. These are they who have the balance and perspective to seek all knowledge – revealed and secular – as a tool and servant for the blessing of themselves and others." (Spencer W. Kimball, *Seek Learning Even by Study and Also by Faith*, Ensign, Sept. 1983, p.3)

Critics of the Church often assert that higher levels of education lead to less devout religious observance. Even within the Church, some members are wary of too much education, fearing they may lose their testimonies. But statistics prove this assertion is false: exactly the opposite occurs within the educated LDS population. Higher levels of education

90

produce higher levels of church activity. Of course there are many exceptions of those who let their intellect smother their faith, but Scott Gordon's research shows that church attendance rates are around 70 to 80 percent among those with sixteen or more years of education.

As a child, I spent many, many hours practicing the piano. Because I grew up in a musical home, I was expected to take my piano studies seriously, but I showed an aptitude for music and quickly excelled. I practiced when my friends were playing on sports teams; I practiced when they were hanging out. I practiced on hotel pianos when on vacation with my family. I practiced when I should have been sleeping. I practiced when my mom was making dinner in the kitchen. I practiced all the time. My parents dedicated our summers to my musical skills by taking me to Los Angeles every summer for eight years so I could study with a teacher there and enter competitions. My mom drove me up and down the East Coast during the school year to local competitions there.

When I entered ninth grade, I supplemented my normal schoolwork by attending the Juilliard School's pre-college program on Saturdays. Juilliard is considered to be the preeminent musical conservatory in the world, and they have a youth program that demands a full Saturday commitment, plus private lessons during the week. I was fully devoted to my piano studies.

In college I continued this dedication, traveling to Italy during my summers to study on music scholarships. And yet with all of that work and focus, I am still not nearly good enough to make a living as a solo concert pianist. I know what that takes – I've seen the talent, sacrifices and discipline of those who do have professional concertizing careers – and I didn't have it.

So was all that work a waste? Was this "secular" training pointless? Should I have assessed my skills early on and said, "I don't have what it takes, so I'm not going to bother?" What was the point of having me compete and train beside the world's best if music wasn't going to be my profession?

I'll never forget crying in my mom's lap after coming in second place in a competition. We were in the privacy of our parked car, and I was about twelve or thirteen at the time. Perhaps I should have been happy with second place, but I was consumed with jealousy for the first place winner: he was my age and studied with my own teacher, but somehow he always seemed to beat me. Even more difficult was that he was my friend, someone I liked outside of competition and hung out with. But he had beaten me yet again, and it was about as much as I could take. Through my tears I wailed, "I hate him! I hate him!" I felt guilty for saying such a thing about a friend, and yet I needed a release for my frustration. I remember the episode as one of the first times I felt truly complicated feelings: jealousy yet admiration for another, a fierce ambition to work even harder yet satisfaction at what I had in fact achieved. Emotional complications such as these are plentiful in our adult lives, and my piano study forced me to confront them early and learn how to deal with them. The episode also promoted spiritual maturity as I learned to love my friend despite his superior piano skills, and as I repented for my cruel words. All this from my "secular" study.

Similarly, the experience of repeatedly performing in front of strangers gave me an arsenal of skills that have served me in adulthood. At around age fourteen or fifteen, I completely forgot the left hand of a Schubert Impromptu as I was performing it in a competition. I played the majority of the piece with just one hand. It remains the most humiliating experience of my life. But after having come through that episode, I feel like I can do anything! Who cares if I fumble my words while giving a talk in church? Who cares if my daughter wears the same dress for three days (and nights)? I survived the Schubert Impromptu! I can survive anything!

Of course, my young career brought some joyful highlights as well: the satisfaction of performing a piece perfectly, the happy sound of hearing my grandpa shout "Bravo!" from the back of an auditorium, the sense of accomplishment at mastering a tricky phrase. Piano has also been my ticket to some amazing spiritual experiences, including playing for President Hinckley at the Jerusalem Center and accompanying an African-American singer in a concert of Negro spirituals. And nothing can rival the gift of being able to accompany my own mother as she sings. My testimony of prayer is strengthened whenever my mom and I kneel before a concert and ask the Lord to imbue our performance with His spirit. The spiritual power of excellent music is one of the keystones of my testimony.

The truth is I never wanted to be a solo concert pianist, and that's not what I was working for. If I had to, yes, I could support myself as a piano teacher or accompanist. But what I got in addition to a professional skill was an amazing tool that I can use throughout my life to promote self fulfillment, bring joy to others and use as a power for good. I love the fact that I am a very good pianist. I like that that defines me. In addition, I now know the amount of work and dedication it takes to rise to the top of any discipline, be it music, academia, or even our spiritual lives. I know from my experience that it takes an almost obsessive pursuit of excellence to achieve greatness, and that includes greatness in our relationships to Christ. I know that high levels of skill in professional or personal lives come as the result of some talent or innate ability, but mostly because of hard work, tenacity and discipline. I learned the truth of President Kimball's statement: "Perspiration must precede inspiration; there must be effort before there is the harvest. We must take thought, work, be patient, acquire competence." (Ensign, Sept 1983) The focus, ambition and maturity I gained from practicing and performing has served me in countless other areas of my life, and even if I never make money playing the piano, this training allowed me to be a fulfilled, hard-working participant in life.

Was my musical education earthly or spiritual? Technically, it was earthly, or secular. But I feel that I received invaluable emotional and spiritual training from it that serves me daily. It most definitely contributed to my testimony and my relationship with Christ. But the rewards of studying a "secular" subject may not always be so obvious. I know as well as anyone how discouraging it can be to spend long hours working or studying and wondering how in the world this tedious work can be promoting my eternal growth. But our rewards for study and learning come in the Lord's time, not ours, and we are building an inner arsenal of power even in our most mundane tasks.

A member of my ward recently worked at the United Nations in New York. There, she witnessed an amazing dialog between a BYU professor and an ambassador of an Islamic country. The professor said to the ambassador, "I have read your Koran and studied its teachings. It is a great book. Now I challenge you to give the same opportunity to the Book of Mormon." And the ambassador did, out of respect for the professor who had taken the time to study his own holy book.

This is a marvelous example of spiritual and earthly educations working together as a power for good. The ambassador allowed the Book of Mormon into his life because the professor had studied the Koran. But I'm not working in the U.N. and you probably aren't either. But we can look beyond that because the principle also applies to the woman who has a Master's Degree but is now sitting behind a computer screen all day or answering phones at an office. It also applies to the woman who studied English Literature or Psychology or Art History in college but is now home with her children. The principle is this: When paired with our spiritual learning, our secular educations are a powerful force for good.

Thus we are told to learn "by study and also by faith." (Doctrine and Covenants 88:118) When we follow this counsel, our earthly educations – whether those educations be in music, academia, or some professional skill—allow us to interact wisely with the world around us. We become more confident, both personally and in our testimonies of Jesus Christ. We are able to make greater contributions to our communities and to our families. We are able to appreciate the beauty of the world around us and find good in all people, rather than living in a spiritual cocoon and shunning all of God's other creations. We find joy in the arts, wonder in the sciences and awe in physical accomplishments. We understand why certain people rise as leaders or as experts in their fields and we can appreciate the quality of their work. And most importantly, we can build characters and intellects that allow God's kingdom on earth to shine as a light on a hill. By balancing curiosity about the world with faith in Christ, we can become more like God. We can grow not just in knowledge and not just in faith, but in intelligence, which is the glory of God, the perfect combination of knowledge and faith. And we can continue to develop both parts of that combination even though we may not be formally enrolled in any educational programs: personal curiosity, scripture study, Sunday meetings, daily interactions with peoples, cultures and sciences allow us to always progress towards intelligence. We can contribute to a culture that represents God's presence here on earth. As young women at the edge of new frontiers, we realize that, even if we release our formal secular educations, we can reclaim all of the curiosity, exuberance, discipline and fulfillment that we discovered during those school years.

Like many of you, I don't have time or money for formal schooling these days. I have officially released my secular education. Instead, I make peanut butter and jelly sandwiches and read *The Very Hungry Caterpiller* eighteen times a day. But I do have a Jewish neighbor and I've been asking her a suspicious number of questions about her Passover celebration. And I do have access to books and magazines and newspapers and other people with whom to share ideas. I participate in book clubs, write and develop my own ideas in a journal, and learn about my husband's professional industry through books, articles and discussions. And my daughter is watching. She's of course watching the way I brush my teeth or unload the dishwasher, and she is inheriting those skills. But she's also inheriting my curiosity. She's inheriting the dedication and energy I put into learning about the world around me, even if it's just learning about the local preschools. She's inheriting my joy at reading a fabulous novel, my satisfaction in a well-written article. She's inheriting my desire to understand what makes art great, or why I always cry at a Mahler symphony. She's inheriting my desire to be an active participant in the lives of others, to serve by adding color and variety to people's lives. She's inheriting my desire to communicate meaningful ideas that help people through difficult times, my desire to be wise at moments of crisis. She's inheriting my desire to master my self, to build character through discipline and productivity. I love this world I'm a part of. It is not my enemy, it does not scare me, and my daughter is inheriting that love.

This, for me, is the legacy of my education. Even now that I'm home full time, I can continue to enjoy the blessings of my time spent in school, and I can reclaim the use of my mind through reading and personal study of subjects I choose. Colored with the lens of the Gospel, education in school or at home gives us control over ourselves and power to shape the world around us. When viewed with this divine perspective, education is no longer a social establishment but rather an attitude of curiosity and reverence for God's creations. It is the means by which we raise righteous families and contribute to our communities. Our educations become not just about creating an earthly career, but creating an eternal character.

Chapter Six

The Do-It-Yourself Church

One Sunday morning, Elliot slumped sleepily in a chair in our bishop's office. It was 6:45am, and a ward council meeting was in progress. The bishop moved to a new agenda item: a discussion on less active families in our ward and how the ward's leaders could help them. The first family on the list to be discussed was the Adamsons, a young couple who was expecting their first child. Did anyone in the room know this family? the bishop asked. Had anyone met with them personally? Did anyone know anything about their personal circumstances? A room of shaking heads answered the bishop's questions.

Elliot's ears perked up as he heard the family's name mentioned. Adamson... Adamson.... Where did he know that name from? Had he met them once at church? Had he heard someone else refer to them? All of a sudden, it dawned on him: he had seen their name on his home teaching assignment list. He was their home teacher. He had been their home teacher for months, but he had never contacted them or met with them. At that moment, Elliot knew that out of the entire ward council, he was the one who was supposed to have stewardship over this family. It should be him answering the bishop's questions, giving a full account of his efforts with the family, his knowledge of their situation, and recommendations for how the ward leaders could help the family become more active. This realization gave Elliot a whopping pit in his stomach, and he sunk down lower in his chair to hide his flushed cheeks. He was ashamed.

***

Soon after the ordination of Pope Benedict XVI, the *New York Times* ran a startling story entitled, "Benedict XVI and the Church That May Shrink. Or May Not." The article proposed that for Benedict XVI's leadership to be successful, he must clearly answer the question most plaguing the Catholic Church: "What do Catholics need to do and believe, in order to truly belong?" (*New York Times*, 29 May 2005) Not definitively answering this question could cause the membership of the Catholic Church to dwindle during Benedict XVI's reign. The article suggested this is because, in a world that enforces no fixed values and in a church that is battling internally over some of its core doctrines, Catholics are unclear on what they *must* do and believe to be in good standing, versus what is recommended.

The article describes the Catholic Church's current confusion:

"The theory and practice [of Catholicism] are very different," said Philip Jenkins, a professor of history and religion at Pennsylvania State University. People tend to belong first to their local parish, then their national church. Local priests and bishops, Professor Jenkins said, often act as buffers against unpopular decisions from the hierarchy.

How important is the core doctrine? What do people need to do to belong? How can the Catholic Church encourage loyalty to the broader church and not just to their local parish? The article suggested that none of these questions is being adequately answered by the Catholic Church at this time. Before becoming a mother, I worked for many years as a marketing manager for a major retail company. Reading this article with my professional marketing hat on, I concluded that the Catholic Church needs to take a fresh look at its brand identity. The Catholic Church is having a brand crisis.

Branding is often a nebulous and confusing concept because it broadly defines a consumer's subconscious reaction to a company or product. If I were to say the word "Nike" to you, you might think of the latest TV commercial, the "swoosh" logo, or perhaps a celebrity sponsor like Michael Jordan. Those are all indicators of the Nike brand which may, whether you realize it or not, prompt you to purchase a Nike product next time you need sneakers. But when I say "Nike", you may also think of tales of sweatshop labor that you heard on the news or how expensive their shoes are or a bad experience you had in one of their stores. These impressions, too, are part of the Nike brand, albeit ones that the company tries to suppress. Ideally, a company's brand sends out a clear, positive message to the consumer, a message that is in harmony with the company's goals. Nike's goal is to provide high-performance shoes for professional and amateur athletes. Understanding this goal, it would be inconsistent for Nike to run a commercial catering to soccer moms, who probably will choose a less expensive, more versatile shoe for their carpooling and errands.

Although "brands" typically refer to our impressions of tangible products like sneakers, organizations also have their own brand identities: companies, schools, symphonies and yes, even churches. So what is the Catholic Church's brand identity? What is the Catholic Church trying to achieve? What are its goals and its strategy for accomplishing those goals? What does the Catholic Church stand for right now? What is it offering its people? What is it requiring of its people? What do Catholics need to do and believe, in order to truly belong? The New York Times article suggested that the Church itself isn't sure.

Of course I ask now, what is the brand identity of the Church of Jesus Christ of Latter-day Saints? President Hinckley asked a similar question in a recent *Ensign* article, entitled "The Symbol of Our Faith". (*Ensign*, April 2005, page 3) He presented the question in the context of a conversation he had with a Protestant minister:

Said [the minister]: "I've been all through [the Mesa Arizona Temple, during the open house period], this temple which carries on its face the name of Jesus Christ, but nowhere have I seen any representation of the cross, the symbol of Christianity. I have noted your buildings elsewhere and likewise find an absence of the cross. Why is this when you say you believe in Jesus Christ?... If you do not use the cross, what is the symbol of your religion?"

Then President Hinckley tells us how he answered that minister's question:

I replied that the lives of our people must become the most meaningful expression of our faith and, in fact, therefore, the symbol of our worship.

From a marketing perspective, President Hinckley made a bold and progressive statement: he suggested that our church does not need a logo – a cross, a swoosh – because our people are themselves the symbol of our brand identity. In fact, we, the members, are the brand. Our product – service, charity, Christ-like lives—speaks for itself. This would be like saying that there is no more accurate and impacting representation of what Nike stands for than the shoe itself, so the shoe is the symbol of the brand.

The swoosh, Michael Jordan, sales people, and the ad agencies are all fired. President Hinckley summarizes:

> No sign, no work of art, no representation of form is adequate to express the glory and the wonder of the Living Christ. He told us what that symbol should be when He said, "If ye love me, keep my commandments" (John 14:15).... And so our lives must become a meaningful expression, the symbol of our declaration of our testimony of the Living Christ, the Eternal Son of the Living God. (*Ensign*, April 2005, page 3)

This optimistic and unequivocal statement by our prophet does not mean that our church organization will never face challenges similar to those currently faced by the Catholic Church. Their organization is considerably larger than ours, and Elder Nelson was recently quoted as saying that the "great concern" of our LDS leadership is the growth of the church. (*Ensign*, June 2005, page 16) Of course we believe that our church will never fall into spiritual confusion because the Savior Himself is guiding it through inspired men, but that doesn't make our organization immune to the challenges of growth. "How can we have our bishops well trained? How can we keep the doctrine pure? How can we keep apostasy from working into the traditions of different wards and branches? That's our great concern," says Elder Nelson.

But there is one element of our organizational structure that separates us from most of the other major religions of the world. This element is one of the great miracles of the restored gospel, a characteristic that helps us avoid some of the trials of the Catholic Church and many other religious organizations. That is the fact that we all serve in the church because we are asked to and because we want to, not because we are paid to.

Our church can be described in many ways: a volunteer organization, a non-profit, a charity, a lay ministry, to name a few. But my favorite description is my own: The Do-It-Yourself Church. This title encompasses, for me, the boot-strapping, down-to-earth everyday religion that we're a part of. While our goals may be noble and nothing short of other-worldly, the real work of our church goes on in the trenches: in the homes of our people, in the Sunday classrooms, in the sleepy early-morning Seminary classes and in the community service projects. We have no paid clergy who can vicariously live good lives for us. There is no one who's getting a paycheck in return for a good Sunday lesson. No one has studied evangelical leadership and is now making a career of it. We are doing it all ourselves.

How does a Do-It-Yourself structure help us avoid some of the pitfalls encountered by other large religious organizations? For one, there is less of an opportunity for pride to corrupt local leaders since our own bishops have not invested the same time, money and personal worth into their roles as professional clergy. If you had spent years of your formal education preparing for the ministry, you might see yourself as quite prepared indeed to lead a congregation, and rightly so. You might have been trained in doctrine as well as in leadership and counseling skills; you would be extremely familiar with your organization's management hierarchy and protocol. You might spend years and years in this professional capacity, gaining a personal insight into your congregation's personality and needs. In contrast, our bishops rarely feel worthy or prepared when their callings come, and the humility that usually accompanies the call prompts a search for help in prayer and in counsel with co-leaders like counselors and Relief Society presidents. We are better fortified to avoid the pitfall described in the *New York Times* article: "People tend to belong first to their local parish, then their national church. Local priests and bishops... often act as buffers against unpopular decisions from the hierarchy."

Another organizational advantage we have in our Do-It-Yourself Church is that we have our leaders living among us, in our midst and more privy to our everyday needs than a professional clergyman might be. After all, this is the way Christ led: As a friend, serving among his people and finding out their needs through ordinary interactions. He didn't make appointments at the temple, waiting for people to come between 2 and 4pm on Saturdays to be taught or healed. Like Christ, the Compassionate Service leader might be your friend and neighbor, which gives her an advantage at knowing your needs over the clergyman who may only see you on Sundays.

Our structure also helps us avoid an "us versus them" mentality, which is so destructive to the concept of a unified, Zion people. We know that if we have complaints with a Relief Society president, we might very well get that same calling ourselves one day -- and then we'll be sorry! This circulation of responsibilities helps avoid situations like the tragic pedophilia crisis in the Catholic Church in which priests are perceived as being loyal to themselves instead of their people.

***

Why is a discussion about the Do-It-Yourself Church important in a book addressed to Mormon women? Because we, as the new generation of servant leaders in the organization, need to realize that the Church will not function and will not fulfill its awesome responsibility unless we do it. The Daughters of Ishmael had to build a civilization out of nothing: each time they moved – from Jerusalem to Bountiful to the Promised Land – they had to provide food, shelter and clothing for themselves and their families. Their experiences in these various places were only what they made them to be. There was no one already there waiting for them with a warm meal and fresh clothing, no one they could pay to build their homes or plant their gardens. They had to create their own circumstances, build their own experiences, as they worked to build the Lord's kingdom. So too do we determine what our experience in the Church will be like. We are the ones responsible for each others' welfare. We are responsible for creating a positive, welcoming environment. We manage the programs, teach the lessons, organize the activities. No one is there to do it for us, no paid clergy to make sure everything runs smoothly and everyone feels welcomed. Just like the Daughters of Ishmael's circumstances were determined by their own labor, so too is our church experience defined by what we put into it.

I believe that the implications of this do not hit us until we are fully entrenched in adulthood, as contributing members of the Church's great service organization, the Relief Society. While growing up in Primary and Young Women, where so many spiritual resources, mentors, leaders and teachers are thrown at us, we may not have fully grasped the demands of the Do-It-Yourself Church. As youth, the parties were always planned for us, the activities meticulously prepared with our spiritual welfare in mind. I experienced amazing youth conferences where my testimony was nurtured by dedicated leaders. Somehow, there were always lessons on Sunday, events on the weekend, and donuts at Seminary. I was certainly grateful for all of the attention, and the system certainly contributed to the growth of my young testimony. But I rarely had to do any of it myself.

I'm sure you, like me, have memories from your childhood of what church service meant in your home: I remember my mom spending hours on the phone in her Relief Society and Primary callings; the casseroles in the freezer, ready at a moment's notice. Perhaps your father spent Wednesday nights in church meetings and wasn't home for dinner. But even if you had great examples of Church service in your home, you were

109

probably on the periphery of truly meaningful service. It was probably not your direct responsibility to help prepare a family for the temple or comfort a sister through a divorce. I encountered some pretty serious problems in my own life and in the lives of my fellow Young Women as I was growing up, but there was always the sense that our leaders were wise, our parents would support us, and Youth Conference would always be cool.

When we leave Young Women, we hit a new frontier: we're no longer the ones being served, but rather the ones doing the serving. We become those wise, supportive leaders ourselves. We have to plan our own activities, teach our own lessons. And if we don't do our visiting teaching, someone feels alone and forgotten. If we don't plan youth conference, it doesn't happen. Or worse: If we don't nurture the young testimonies in our Primary students, maybe they're lost. There are no nurturing Young Women's leaders to pick up the slack.

This transition from being served to doing the serving can be more challenging than we might anticipate. After graduating from a fantastic youth program in my home ward and stake, I felt awkward going to Relief Society in my college ward, where most of the women were wives of graduate students or graduate students themselves. With few undergraduate women in the ward, I felt like there wasn't really a place for me. Lessons focused on motherhood, building homes, combating loneliness. I missed the exuberant attention of my Young Women leaders. But in my junior year of college, I was called to be in the Relief Society presidency, and my whole world changed. I was forced to release the feeling of entitlement that had dominated my experience as a youth in the Church – the sense that everything would be organized for me and with my welfare in mind – and claim instead a new attitude: it was now my turn to work on behalf of others. My eyes were opened to the opportunity of service, an opportunity which I hadn't known how to grasp during my first two years within the women's organization. Taking cues from my inspired president, I dedicated myself to serving the new young women who were entering the Relief Society and feeling out of place like I had. I developed a profound love and concern for them, and by developing friendships with them, praying about them, and counseling with my Relief Society president, I learned how to serve them.

I believe we do need *to learn* how to serve. Faith in Action, Personal Progress and the other youth programs do a good job of creating opportunities to serve and teaching us the rewards of service, through personal and group goal setting as well as community projects. But as adults, the needs of others are rarely pointed out to us with such fanfare. It takes practice to see that a sister is inwardly suffering or to know that a family needs support. It takes courage to offer babysitting to a mother when she's never asked for help, or to bring food to a family who appears not to be hungry. We need to release the attitude that our fellow church members are there to serve us; we instead need to be there to serve them. By praying for inspiration we can tune ourselves into the promptings of the Spirit, but we still need to practice listening to those promptings, acting on them, and putting aside any personality quirks that may cause us not to notice the needs of others. We need to practice sitting next to someone new every week in Relief Society, inviting someone new to join our playgroup, or listening to friends in a new way so that we hear their real needs, not just the normal chitchat.

For me, it took a formal calling in the Relief Society of my college ward to give me the practice I needed. But you might find another way to release the self-centeredness of youth and exercise your serving spirit. There are numerous organized outlets for service in the Church, including the Bishop's Storehouse, Enrichment activities, temple service, moving and cleaning opportunities, performance opportunities and every single calling that exists. The entire church organization, regardless of your specific calling, acts as an instrument by which we work together to serve God. The inspired organization of the Church, our Do-It-Yourself Church, allows us to rise to the calling of being God's servants and challenges us to manage His Kingdom on earth. While the Church is often a place that exemplifies Christlike virtues of love and service, it is *always* a place to practice them.

My favorite metaphor for the Do-It-Yourself Church is that of a fitness gym. You don't get the benefits simply by joining. And no one can lose weight or tone your muscles for you. Instead, the real reward comes from using the machines yourself, preferably several different machines, and especially the machines which you're naturally not good at. In our youth programs, we are shown the machines by fit and admirable personal trainers. The machines' mechanisms are explained and we learn about the impacted muscle groups. We participate in group training sessions that are scheduled so that it's embarrassing if we miss one.

But as an adult, the group training sessions are less frequent. It is now our responsibility to go to the gym ourselves, to motivate ourselves, and practice those things that might be challenging to us. If we pay for our gym membership but don't take advantage of the machines, our names remain in the computers but our muscles atrophy and we get pudgy. Similarly, if we don't take advantage of the formal and informal service opportunities in the Church, our spiritual muscles don't receive the revitalizing effects of true Church membership.

Another favorite metaphor for our relationship to the church is that of a "consumer" and a "producer". Once, at the funeral of a truly great man, I heard Elder Neal A. Maxwell praise this man as a "gospel producer", stating that this is a quality most appreciated by the Church's leadership. By this compliment, Elder Maxwell meant that this man had produced all good things in his service in the Church: faith in himself and in others, organizational leadership in his callings, service to those in need. He had led a life of productive service and had needed or expected little in return. But as part of his compliment, Elder Maxwell contrasted this man to a "gospel consumer", or someone who relies too heavily on the goodness of Church members and doesn't contribute equally in spiritual or temporal ways. Eliza R. Snow gently chided "gospel consumers" in her song, "Think not, When You Gather to Zion": "Think not when you gather to Zion,/ The Saints here have nothing to do/ But to look to your personal welfare,/ And always be comforting you." (*Hymns*, 1948. p. 21) Amusing, but still true.

Someone who properly understands the Do-It-Yourself Church is by nature a "gospel producer". It is an epitaph we should all strive for.

For a more elevated discussion of our purpose in the Do-It-Yourself Church, I turn to Truman Madsen and an address he gave at BYU Education Week in 1973. In his own beautiful way, he describes the difference between just joining the gym and actually using the machines:

One supreme compliment to a member of the Church is, "He is active." But so are falling rocks and billiard balls. The word the Lord uses, and the question derived from it is, "Are you a *lively* member?" Are you alive?

...In recent years the Church has set many new attendance records. But how nourished are those who are within the Church buildings?

...Some of us do "100 percent home teaching." But do we leave in the home a living atmosphere?

What good is a woman, I am sometimes asked, who has done almost nothing for years "except hold a family together"? That is all. The Lord's answer is that if she has created and transmitted the nutriments of spiritual life in her home..., then she has been the purveyor of life. And nothing is more crucial!

Suppose we go to the temple and (how impotent the phrase!) "do names." Actually we are bringing new birth and life to spirit personalities whose exquisite gratitude, according to the Prophet Joseph Smith, will be such that they will fall to our knees and embrace them and bathe our feet with their tears. That is what we are about....

The time may come when we don't just "say a blessing" on the food but when we, in effect, seek to make every act of our lives life-giving and done in the Lord's name and with his Spirit. Then the whole earth and the whole day and the whole of our lives will be the temple within which we labor with and for him. (*The Highest in Us,* 28)

What I love about this passage is that Madsen takes many of our familiar phrases that we use to describe service in the Church – "active", "100 percent home teaching", "hold a family together", "do names", and "say a blessing" – and opens to us the true divinity of these common actions. In the Do-It-Yourself Church, we get to do each of these ourselves. No one is paid to do them for us. We receive all of the blessings. We have the opportunity to have "the whole earth and the whole day and the whole of our lives...be the temple within which we labor with and for him." What an amazing way to live. And it is within our grasp.

But as servants within the Do-It-Yourself Church, we also have our own unique challenges. These challenges may be different from those faced by paid ministries, but they are just as damaging. Madsen's passage suggests that even "active" members can fall short of being "alive," meaning that they can perform their duties but without the liveliness that defines a life in Christ. If epidemic, this lack of "alive" service can cause us as a people to descend into apathy. And apathy leads to mediocrity. And there is no place for mediocrity in the Lord's kingdom on earth.

So often in our worldly culture, performance is directly correlated to compensation. A person is more likely to do a better job at a task if he is paid more. In our consumer culture, we have a hard time seeing beyond the monetary reward. But in the Church, we are challenged to look far beyond our earthly paradigms of career and compensation. We are challenged instead to look at eternal rewards and to work for the greater good of the Lord's Kingdom rather than for our own personal advancement. But sometimes this divine compensation is just too distant to really get us motivated, and good people who do exceptional work in their professional lives find themselves preparing a half-hearted talk in the hall before Sacrament Meeting. One of the great red flags of the Do-It-Yourself Church is this: Our volunteer service is not a free pass to mediocrity.

When we receive a call in the Church that doesn't come naturally to us – perhaps it's a machine at the gym that exercises some previously unused muscle – we too often excuse ourselves from doing a good job. We might tell ourselves "This isn't a good time for me to have this calling," or "I don't have anything to offer." And usually we can get away with doing pretty little because we won't get demoted or fired and because our performance is rarely criticized by understanding ward members. The motivation to do a good job – no, to do an excellent job– must come from our relationship with Christ and from our understanding of what it means to be an "alive" member of the Church.

We cannot go to church expecting to be bored. But too often, we do. This creeping characteristic of our people can be just as insidious as if we stopped attending altogether. If the teacher isn't providing an excellent lesson, it is our job to turn it into one. That is part of our responsibility in the Do-It-Yourself Church. Why is it important for our meetings to be excellent? Because in them we worship our God, we edify each other and we teach our children. But also because they are the best indicator of our culture as a people. Do we want to be a culture of excellence? We have to be. Brigham Young explained it this way:

> We have an object in view, and that is to gain influence among all the inhabitants of the earth for the purpose of establishing the Kingdom of God in its righteousness, power and glory, and to exalt the name of Deity, and cause that name by which we live to be revered everywhere that he may be honored, that his works may be honored, that we may be honored ourselves, and deport ourselves worth of the character of his children. (*Discourses of Brigham Young*, 438-39)

Brigham Young reminds us of what President Hinckley told the inquiring Protestant Minister: We, the members, are the representation of the Church and the God that leads it. We are to "cause that name by which we live to be revered everywhere." No one is trained and hired to do it for us.

As some of the youngest members of Relief Society, we young adult women are the servant leaders that will take our Church into the future. We are servants because we do the work of Jesus Christ, our Lord and Savior. We serve our families at home, we serve our sisters in Relief Society, we serve our wards in callings and we serve in our communities. Our servant-hood is the essence of membership in the Church, the means by which we exercise our spirits and train for divinity. But we are also leaders because we labor within a Do-It-Yourself organization that depends on us to fulfill its purpose. We determine the character of our meetings and the quality of our people. Our ability and willingness to lead makes the Church what it is, and in turn, makes God's Kingdom what it is. In Brigham Young's words, we define the character of God's Kingdom on earth; we influence how "all the inhabitants of the earth" view and understand our God; we "exalt the name of Diety" and we are responsible for the "character of his children." Leave it to Brigham Young to say it best.

***

So what happened to Elliot and the Adamsons, that family he was supposed to be home teaching? Fortunately, the story has a very happy ending. Elliot left that ward council meeting reminded of his responsibility in the Do-It-Yourself Church. He recognized that if he, their home teacher, didn't make an effort with them, no one would. He had been given stewardship over this family and that stewardship gave him the power to change their lives.

He and I together visited the Adamsons in their home. We learned about why they were in San Francisco, what their interests were, what their families were like. We learned about complications in the wife's pregnancy, unhappiness at the husband's job. We learned that the couple had a desire to become reactivated at church, but that they felt shy and out of place.

Over time as our friendship developed, we learned that they had a desire to go to the temple and be sealed together. Within a year, the Adamsons had a supportive group of friends at church who encouraged them in this goal and helped them set a date. Elliot volunteered to teach temple preparation discussions in their home. I will never forget those discussions: Elliot and I meeting with the Adamsons in their apartment eating Chinese take-out while we outlined for them what they would experience in the Lord's house. This was truly the gospel in action, and we had the opportunity to be a part of it.

Elliot and I were invited to the Adamson's sealing in the Los Angeles temple. Sister Adamson's grandfather officiated, with faithful families from both sides surrounding them. For me and Elliot, that sealing was a vision of what miracles can happen when we simply do our jobs.

At a family dinner after the sealing, their parents approached me and Elliot. Tears streamed down their faces. Brother Adamson's father took us each by the hand and said, "We prayed that someone would take the time to seek out our children. You were the answer to our prayers because you were willing to magnify your calling as their home teachers. Thank you." We insisted that it was we who were thankful for the blessings of the Do-It-Yourself Church.

CHAPTER SEVEN
THE HAVE-IT-ALL MYTH

I recently received a mailing from the all girls' school I attended for twelve years while growing up in New York. It was the school's annual fundraising plea, and so the pages of the glossy brochure were filled with the school's most prestigious and powerful alumnae: Christy Todd Whitman, former governor of New Jersey and Director of the EPA was pictured on the cover. Inside were pictures of female partners at law firms, the head of an inner city hospital's surgical unit, a successful author and various other politicians. It was, to be sure, an impressive display of the heights women can reach today in their chosen careers. These women are contributing to our communities and our country in important ways, and their contributions were made possible by the generations before us who fought for education and opportunities in the workplace.

After I'd flipped through the pages and read the brief bios, I passed the brochure to Elliot over dinner. But I wasn't asking him to marvel at the accomplished women. Instead I asked, "Where's the mother? Where's the woman who's home with her three kids?" Of course, it was a rhetorical question: we both knew that no woman would be featured in this fancy brochure for "just" being a mother. Perhaps some of the women pictured did have children, but that alone did not qualify them to be featured. They had to have done something powerful, something public, and motherhood was too ordinary to qualify.

I wondered aloud to Elliot what my girls' school would do if, hypothetically, I were to offer a large sum of money to endow a course on motherhood. Perhaps it would be a history course that would look at the varying behaviors and customs of mothers throughout the ages. Perhaps it would be a sociology course, focusing on Dr. Spock and other various mothering styles popular in the 20th Century. Perhaps it would be a literature course in which students would read novels with motherly heroines. My only requisite would be that the course would have to focus on what it means to be a mother.

My point in imagining this hypothetical situation was that in the twelve years I attended the school, from first grade through twelfth grade, the subject of motherhood – or the fact that many if not most of us girls would be mothers at some point in our lives – never entered our classroom discussion. I loved my school and being educated only with women gave me confidence and a sense of womanly power which I may not have adopted in different circumstances; I was taught that I could do anything, be anything. But these encouragements and empowerments were always presented in the context of professional life. I was training my mind and my sense of self so that I could be a better doctor or lawyer or even a better social worker. Not so that I would be a better mother. Not so that we would be better prepared to raise society's future generation.

If I offered my endowment gift today, I don't think my school would accept it. I think the focus of women's education today is still too much focused on professional development to admit that a good percentage of women are mothers-in-training. However, I have a feeling that possibly in only five or ten years from now, my gift might be considered differently and possibly even accepted. I anticipate a change in priorities and focus in our broad American culture that might make such a gift appealing to my school.

Why am I so optimistic? Why do I think the role of motherhood will come to the fore of a woman's education in so brief a time? Because a wave of newspaper articles, magazine articles, books and conversations with non-Mormon women suggest to me that there is a crisis in play among women of our generation who were taught that they could "have it all": they could be that doctor, that lawyer, that teacher, that social worker, and still have a happy and fulfilling family life all at once. That crisis is the realization that none of the factors influencing a modern woman's life -- society, government, workplaces, schools, nor our inner female psyches—is built to support having it all. Despite the years of schooling and noble efforts of our foremothers, many American mothers today just can't seem to find a way to be a good mother, a good worker, a good wife and a happy individual all at once. Many women now feel betrayed.

The efforts of our foremothers in the 1960's and '70s succeeded in opening the educational and professional opportunities available to women. By 1986, a majority of all women with children under age three were in the workforce. (*Perfect Madness*, 89) But social institutions such as day care and part-time work programs didn't adapt to accommodate those women who either had to or wanted to work. Quality day care was expensive and hard to come by, and part-time work was scarce and unequally rewarded. Instead of catching up to the demands of the modern working mother, institutions and workplaces remained inflexible in their policies, and day care became more expensive. By the 1990s, the working mother started becoming skeptical of her ability to have happy children, pay her bills, remain close to her husband, and thrive in a professional environment all at once. But, these women told themselves, this is what I was promised. This is what I deserve as a modern woman. This is what my education prepared me for. Why, then, is it so darn hard? Why aren't I happy? Why can't I have it all and keep my sanity?

This disillusionment with the have-it-all myth of our generation's youth started exhibiting itself through our popular culture in the 1990s. The 1990s was the age of Martha Stewart, when all of a sudden it became cool again to invest in your home life and simply in making things beautiful. In retail, the '90s saw the rise of Pottery Barn and Williams-Sonoma and other so-called "nesting" stores where women and families both browsed and bought in urges of domesticity. *Real Simple* and other domestic magazines popularized do-it-yourself interior decorating and at-home projects. The term "soccer mom" came into existence in the political races of 1996, and all of a sudden there was a new modern woman: the woman who took pride in carpooling her kids to soccer, getting involved with homework and over scheduling after-school activities. The growing pains of this era were crystallized by Marilyn Quayle's 1992 speech in which she stated that mothers did not want to be liberated from their "essential natures as women", contrasted with Hillary Rodham Clinton's infamous statement about how she could have "stayed home and baked cookies".

Within the past ten years since the advent of the soccer mom, more and more women have thrown themselves into the profession of motherhood, rather than pursuing the paid jobs that their advanced degrees might have prepared them for. But the battle within women continues, and a wave of recent books addresses the crisis that continues to bubble underneath the surface and make modern American women dissatisfied. In October 2003, the *New York Times Magazine* ran a cover story titled "The Opt-Out Revolution" which featured a number of women who had opted out of their formerly high-powered careers in favor of staying home with their kids. They expressed joy at spending more time with their children, but frustration at not being able to pursue their professional interests in more depth. Even the most educated, well-trained women – the women who were supposed to "take rightful ownership of the universe", as the article stated – could not be successful workers and successful mothers at the same time. Even *they* had to choose. This article opened the floodgates to a public and heated discussion on the betrayal of the have-it-all myth. In 2005's *Perfect Madness*, Judith Warner calls the modern American mother's situation "this mess." She goes on to define the mess: "This caught-by-the-throat feeling so many mothers have today of *always* doing something wrong....This widespread, choking cocktail of guilt and anxiety and resentment and regret is poisoning motherhood for American women today.... An existential discomfort." In *The Mommy Wars*, a 2006 best selling collection of essays contrasting working mothers and stay-at-home mothers, each essay contributor espouses the virtues of her chosen lifestyle with a moral vehemence that betrays the frustration and anxiety of both sides. Most recently, Linda Hirshman in *Get to Work* says a woman must have a career outside the home to "have work that brings you influence, honor, compensation, a way of being political and a hand in shaping the world." *Newsweek* featured the book in a recent issue, and the angry letters-to-the-editor suggest that Hirshman's position is not popular. (*Newsweek*, July 3-10, 2006)

This latest wave of public conversation about the emotional health of American mothers has created an awareness and appreciation for mothers that hasn't existed in our culture for many decades. We as a culture are now talking about what goes on in our homes, how mothers play critical roles in the upbringing of children, and why some women are happier being mothers than others. There is a focus on the frustration and disillusionment that plagues so many modern American mothers, and an effort to solve them. Feminism has long dominated the academic study of women. But now we are seeing Motherhood rise as a new accepted academic discipline, a subject worthy of being studied by sociologists, psychologists and historians alike.

This is why I am optimistic about my school accepting my hypothetical proposal for a course on motherhood: Because now more than ever before in my lifetime, the challenges facing modern mothers, the importance of mothers, and the personal fulfillment of mothers are topics of mainstream discussion in the media and even among academicians.

***

But does this new cultural discussion on motherhood apply to Mormon mothers? Can we relate to the "mess" described in *Perfect Madness*, or the frustration of the "opt-out revolution"? Do we too feel betrayed by the have-it-all myth?

We are, after all, modern American mothers ourselves and welcome participants in this current public discussion. But what is different about us? Do our beliefs exempt us from the frustrations felt by some of our non-Mormon mothering peers?

Perhaps because of my schooling but mostly because of my emotional health after the birth of my first daughter, I decided to go back to work. I knew the spiritual importance of being home with my children, but I was not happy. With only one child at home and an ache to return to the workplace, I figured this was the perfect time to try to "have it all": I would find a part-time job that kept my mind active while still nurturing my child and excelling in my role as a wife. It was a perfect plan, accommodating all of my various roles yet being true to what I believed was important.

I hired a wonderful young mother in my ward to tend Esme, and I found an exciting position as the marketing director for a children's clothing company where I could work three days a week. What could be better? I thought. I was even working with products for kids! My worlds were meshing, my daughter was thriving and I was happy.

Except that my perfect situation soon disintegrated. About ten months later, the job ended in one of those I Quit/You're Fired dances where everyone's unhappy but no one's sure what went wrong. In hindsight, I see that I became less and less satisfied at work because I felt my bosses had misled me: they had promised me (and were paying me for) a three-day-a-week job, yet they burdened me with a workload suitable for several full-time employees. I felt overwhelmed and unable to do my best work. They, in turn, resented my unwillingness to work more on the days I wasn't in the office. I tried to be principled in my approach to part-time work ("This is my work time and this is my family time.") and that didn't fly with them.

I was bitterly disappointed and frustrated. I had only one child, terrific childcare, a supportive and loving husband, a good education, a good work ethic... and yet I still wasn't able to have it all. Wasn't I supposed to be able to make it all work? Hadn't I been promised that as a modern American woman that I could have my family, my work and my self all at once? Had I failed? Had I been betrayed?

At this low point, I could have very easily joined with the other American mothers who bemoan "this mess" of modern motherhood. I would have let my sense of failure eat at my confidence, convincing me that I had indeed failed at everything my education and upbringing had prepared me for. I would have convinced myself that I hadn't worked hard enough and wasn't tough enough to balance work and family. But perhaps I would have also blamed a work culture that didn't protect part-time workers like me and that expected me to work even on my days at home. Perhaps I would have pursued a new job, not part time but full time, in an effort to prove to myself and my peers that I really do have what it takes. Perhaps I would have hung on to the have-it-all myth and convinced myself that my happiness would still come from splitting my time and my energies.

But this didn't happen. Instead, I brushed off my ego, bought memberships to every children's museum, zoo and aquarium in the city, and dedicated myself to being the best darn mom I could possibly be. Instead of relying on the have-it-all gospel to bring me happiness, I decided to exercise faith in the divine role of mothers. Staying home full time was and still is a tough transition for me, filled with lonely and frustrating moments and cravings for the life I left behind. But my personal satisfaction is greatly increased by knowing that I am doing one thing – the most important thing – very well, rather than a lot of things sort of well.

What is different about my experience than, say, another modern American mother who might struggle with the have-it-all myth? It is, of course, my belief in the divinity of motherhood and my conviction that, having to choose between a self-gratifying paid career and the career of motherhood, choosing motherhood will always be choosing the better part. My failed attempt to "have it all" allowed me to develop my testimony of motherhood and to truly practice what I believed, even though it doesn't necessarily come naturally to me.

And soon motherhood became fulfilling at least, if still not natural. I've broken free of the mantra that personal stimulation equals paid work. I no longer believe that I have to receive a paycheck to be validated. Instead, I've become satisfied with living a more internal life, a life in which reading a good book in my limited spare time is just as fulfilling as thinking through a marketing strategy. My addiction to external praise and performance feedback waned as my child became my only audience and I my only critic. It's easy to go to an office, get paid, and feel like we've done something. It takes far more initiative to create rich and impacting lives at home.

And this is what we Mormon women can add to the public dialogue on motherhood that is now coming to the fore: that motherhood can be enough. It can be enough to fulfill us as women; it can be enough for us as members of a liberated modern society. We do not need to do more or be more to prove our worth to ourselves or to others. We as members of the Church have the *Proclamation on the Family*. We have our beliefs in the eternal nature of family and in the importance of motherhood. We know we have a sacred calling. We know how tough motherhood is, even without having to worry about external paid jobs or any other complicating aspect of modern life. These convictions make us unique and they validate our role as mothers in a way that society never will, even with all the current books and articles on the subject. Womanhood can be satisfied in motherhood. We don't have to prove ourselves in other ways. This can be our message to mothers who are under the spell of the have-it-all myth.

It has been the message of many Mormon mothers for generations before us. It's nothing new or revolutionary. But in this generation – our generation – this message has the potential to be more powerful than ever before. Because of the increased cultural wars in our country over the purpose and definition of family, because of the dialogue on motherhood that is now entering mainstream media, and because of the confusion and sometimes suffering of our non-Mormon maternal peers, our message can be a source of comfort and direction to many. Our message tells mothers that they don't have to beat themselves up if they don't want to hold down a job while raising a family. Our message lets mothers admit that "having it all" is overrated and harder than it looks. Our message tells mothers who have to work to support their families that we are in awe of them. Our message gives mothers the courage to opt-out of the have-it-all myth without feeling like a failure.

Our message also celebrates the mother as a woman, giving her the right to invest in herself as an individual and as a daughter of God. In believing that motherhood is enough to fulfill our potential as women, we free mothers from society's demands and expectations and give them the time and the confidence to celebrate themselves. We place a high value on emotional health, on developing talents and on pursuing interests that make us happy and fulfill our intellectual and emotional needs. We're free to enforce "quiet time" at home so we can spend some precious time on our own interests. We're free to go on trips with our husbands, to take a class that intrigues us. A friend recently recalled to me how, when she was in high school and her other siblings already away from home, her mother returned to work part-time in their local school district. But her mother worked for months before my friend even found out about it – and even then she heard about it from a neighbor! Perhaps my friend was out of touch with her mother, but just as significant is the fact that the mother did not share of herself with her daughter. I instead prefer to have my daughter know the whole me, not just the mommy me. I make an effort to tell my daughter what I do whenever we're apart. I want her to know me not only as her mother, but as a whole woman with passions and abilities outside of my devotion to her. I want her to respect me as an individual, as a daughter of Heavenly Father myself, as a competent and capable woman even though I am not being financially rewarded by working outside the home.

As part of our message, we can acknowledge that life is long, full of various seasons that free mothers from the strictures of the conventional career path. We don't have to spend our twenties and thirties climbing up professional ladders as so many of our peers are expected to. We believe that we can in fact "have it all" – just not simultaneously as the myth promises. Mormon mothers often return to school or go to work or go on missions in the later years of our motherhood, taking advantage of life's natural rhythm more effectively than those who work through their best childbearing years.

President Faust prophetically declared our message twenty years ago in a 1986 *Ensign* article. His words came at the height of women's involvement in the workplace, but they resonate perhaps even more today as non-Mormon women look for the validation they need to prioritize motherhood above their careers:

> Women today are being encouraged by some to have it all—generally, all simultaneously: money, travel, marriage, motherhood, separate careers in the world....
>
> Doing things sequentially – filling roles one at a time at different times – is not always possible, as we know, but it gives a woman the opportunity to do each thing well in its time and to fill a variety of roles in her life. A woman... may fit more than one career into

the various seasons of life. She need not try to sing all the verses of her song at the same time. (*Ensign*, Sept. 1986, 18-19.)

I still struggle daily with the meaning and scope of my role as mother. Some mornings, I feel my daughter by the side of my bed gently prodding me awake and something in me rebels and wants to crawl under the covers. But other times, I stare into her radiant face and can't imagine being anything besides her mother. To those of you for whom motherhood comes more naturally, congratulations. You have a gift that I do not. As I write this, I am two weeks away from having my second child, and I pray daily for peace and courage to get through this next transition. But what keeps me going is my testimony of our message, our gospel's message of motherhood. I believe President Faust's words, and I believe our doctrine of the divine role of mothers. Although I sometimes feel frustrated and envious of those with more external lives, I know from my personal experience that trying to have it all isn't the perfect solution it's promised to be.

***

Like many of you, I learned to value motherhood from my own mother. But, paradoxically, it was precisely because my mother worked the entire time I was growing up that I came to appreciate motherhood. My mother is an extremely gifted and hard-working opera singer, and the

Lord gave her opportunities early in her life to develop a professional career that many only dream of. She seized these opportunities, magnified her talents and rose to the height of her profession. However, the Lord did not bless her with equally rich opportunities to be a mother. Being one of five children herself she wanted several children, but when it came time to bear them, I was the only child she was able to successfully deliver.

Because of her career, my mother has been able to represent the Church and be an example of the Gospel to untold numbers of people. She has touched people with the Spirit as she sings and communicates with others in a totally unique way. I have always loved the fact that my mother works – that she has this whole other life outside of me in which she is able to fulfill herself and do good. I am intensely proud of her, in awe of her skills, and am always trying to be like her.

Throughout the '80s and '90s as I was growing up, my mother gave dozens of firesides and talks throughout the Church on "having it all." As a professional and a mother, she was, in fact, having it all – family, career, faith – and she served as an inspiring role model to Mormon women everywhere. But what allowed my mother to touch Mormon audiences was that she never preached the have-it-all myth as I was taught it in school or as it is touted in the popular media. She never claimed she could do everything well *all at one time*. What she taught instead was balance: she was the first to admit that she had made sacrifices – a little here and a little there – to have the rich life she did. She only had one child, for starters, which in itself put her in a unique camp among

Mormon mothers. Her husband, my father, was not an active member of the Church and they did not have a temple marriage, so that too added a unique dimension to her situation. Also, her job did not keep her away from home the same way a corporate position would; a lot of her work was done at home memorizing music, and when she was "at work", it was often at night during a performance that was after my bedtime. In addition, she was able to involve me in her work, bringing me to rehearsals and, when I got older, even to performances where I would knit clothes for my Cabbage Patch Kids with the opera house's make-up and costume artists in the backstage dressing rooms.

And so my mom was always the first to admit that she was not living the life of a typical Mormon mother. She never told Mormon mothers they could be like her or that they too could have successful jobs while being successful mothers. What she did tell them was that, despite the glamour of her profession and the ability she had to be a unique missionary for the church, her most treasured role was that of mother. She told her audiences that, even though she only had one child at home, she chose not to magnify her career even more by traveling and performing internationally because it was important that she be home for me. She told her audiences that I was her "five-in-one" – that she had really wanted five children but that Heavenly Father gave her all five just in me. The few times I saw my mother lose her usual elegance was when some insensitive Church member would assume she had wanted "only" one child and would imply that my mother was inferior to more typical Mormon mothers with more kids.

And so, in her way, my mother revised the have-it-all myth for Mormon women a generation ago by revealing that in order to have it all, there must be sacrifices. She sacrificed a more prominent career because she wanted to be home with me. Heavenly Father's plan for her forced her to sacrifice the large Priesthood-bearing family she had anticipated, and, she acknowledged, that is not a sacrifice Mormon women typically want to or are forced to make. And when childbearing proved to be easy for me, I knew it was not a sacrifice I was willing to make either. For myself, for my mom, for my belief in eternal families, I want to have the children my mom never had. I remind myself of this whenever I struggle with letting go of my own have-it-all dreams. I will never be my mother: I don't have her rare professional gifts. But she is not me: I'm growing a larger, more typical family. Neither of us will ever have it all. But what we have is enough.

ABOUT THE AUTHOR

Neylan McBaine's writing has been published in *Newsweek*, *Dialogue: A Journal of Mormon Thought*, *Segullah*, *Meridian Magazine*, PowerofMoms.com and BustedHalo.com. She serves as the Personal Voices editor for *Dialogue* and writes a regular column for Patheos.com, a premier religious information portal.

Neylan is the founder and editor-in-chief of The Mormon Women Project, a continuously expanding library of interviews with Latter-day Saint women found at www.mormonwomenproject.com.

WORKS CITED

Annan, Kofi. As quoted by Educate Girls Globally. http://www.educategirls.org/index.htm, 2006.

Belkin, Lisa. "The Opt-Out Revolution." *The New York Times Magazine*, October 26, 2003.

Conference Report, Oct. 1962, 59-60

Dobriansky, Paula. As quoted in *The Education of Girls in the Developing World.* UNGEI Press Release, September 29, 2006.

Faust, James E. "A Message to My Granddaughters: Becoming 'Great Women.'" *Ensign*, September 1986.

Fisher, Ian. "Benedict XVI and the Church That May Shrink. Or Not." *The New York Times*, 29 May 2005.

Gordon, Scott. *Education, Scholarship and Mormonism*, from www.fairlds.org, 2006.

Hinckley, Gordon B. "The Symbol of our Faith," *Ensign*, April 2005.

Hirshman, Linda. *Get To Work.* New York: Viking Adult, 2006.

Hymns of the Church of Jesus Christ of Latter-day Saints. Salt Lake City: The Church of Jesus Christ of Latter-day Saints, 1948.

Kimball, Spencer W. *The Teachings of Spencer W. Kimball*, ed. Edward L Kimball, 1982.

Kimball, Spencer W. "Seek Learning Even by Study and Also by Faith." *Ensign*, September 1983.

Letters to the Editor. *Newsweek.* July 3-10, 2006.

Madsen, Truman. *The Highest in Us*. Salt Lake City: Bookcraft,1978.

National Vital Statistics System: Marriages and Divorces fact sheet, from http://www.cdc.gov/nchs/nvss.htm, 2005.

Nelson, Russell M. "The Mission and Ministry of the Savior: A Discussion with Elder Russell M. Nelson" *Ensign*, June 2005.

Richardson, Matthew O. "Three Principles of Marriage." *Ensign*, April 2005.

Steiner, Leslie Morgan. *The Mommy Wars*. New York: Random House, 2006.

Warner, Judith. *Perfect Madness*, New York: Riverhead, 2006.

Young, Brigham. *Discourses of Brigham Young*. Selected by John A. Widtsoe. 1941.

Made in the USA
Las Vegas, NV
15 August 2021

28230441R00083